Copyright ©
ISBN 978-0-915545-21-6
First Printing 2014

Printed in the United States of America
All Rights Reserved!

Published by
Stanley R. Abbott Ministries, Inc.
P.O. Box 533
McRae, Georgia 31055
U.S.A.

The cover, *Jesus Healing the Sick,* is an illustration from
The Dore Gallery of Bible Illustrations by Gustave Dore
taken from the Public Domain.
Gustave Dore 1832 - 1883

Lord of Healing

Preface

Modern societies have made tremendous advances in life. Technologies are operational that were not even dreams in our recent past! We barely have our new cell phone activated, and there is already a new version available. Cyberspace has changed the world. The medical community continues to perfect surgical procedures even transplanting tissue from a cadaver into a living human. Researchers can now artificially grow stem cells for possible use as various tissues such as muscles or nerves. The breakthroughs in medicine are staggering.

Although some diseases are touted as having been eradicated, other diseases such as HIV, or the new flu strains H5N1 or H7N9 surface with regularity. In Wikipedia's section on the Pharmaceutical Industry they quote IMS *(Market Prognosis International)* estimating the 2011 global spending on prescription drugs topped $954 billion. Without being a cynic I believe it is safe to say infirmities, sicknesses, and diseases are going to be a part of this world as long as Satan is the *"...ruler of this world..." **(John 16:11)***.

What provision does God have for His sons to be able to deal with infirmities, sicknesses, and diseases? There seem to be as many doctrines about this subject in the *"...church..."* as there are people. We must have *"...sound doctrine..."* regarding the will of God in this matter! This book is written as a glimpse into the will of God regarding healing hoping to *"...provoke..."* the sons of God to study to show themselves approved unto God so they may see this holy provision of healing! ***I pray it works...***

Lord of Healing

Table of Contents

Chapter One
The Lamb's Blood — 1 - 12

Chapter Two
Why? — 13 - 22

Chapter Three
Appropriating Healing — 23 - 36

Chapter Four
Doubt's Effects on Faith — 37 - 48

Chapter Five
Laying on of Hands — 49 - 56

Chapter Six
Faith to Receive — 57 - 64

Chapter Seven
Patience to Receive   65 - 74

Chapter Eight
Diversity of Methods   75 - 84

Chapter Nine
What if..."   85 - 94

Chapter Ten
Spirits of Infirmity   95 - 104

Summary & Conclusion   105 - 107

Chapter One

The Lamb's Blood

At the conclusion of the sixth day of creation Scripture says, *"...Then God saw everything that He had made, and indeed it was very good..." (Genesis 1:31)*. There was no sin and no death in any of the things God made in those six days; everything was full of light and life. Adam and Eve were in an environment God called *"...very good..."*: A place in which they were intended to live and not die *(Genesis 1`:26-28)*.

However, Adam's treasonous disobedience of what he knew to be the will of God caused *"...sin and death..."* to enter creation.

> *"...through one man (Adam) sin entered the world, and death through sin, and thus death spread to all men..."*
> **Romans 5:12**

Adam was not deceived *(I Timothy 2:14)* as was Eve *(II Corinthians 11:3)*. Adam yielded to sin of his own volition, an act of his free will. Scripture says,

> *"Do you not know that to whom you present yourselves slaves to obey, you are that one's slaves whom you obey, whether of sin leading to death, or of obedience leading to righteousness?"* **Romans 6:16**

Adam's yielding to sin caused him to become a slave of sin leading to his death and passing death on to all men.

Lord of Healing

God's kingdom is a kingdom of light and life. The kingdom where Satan rules is a kingdom of darkness and death. It is important to present these contrasts as revelation taught in Scripture inspired by God the Holy Spirit.

> *"...**God is light and in Him is no darkness at all**..."*
> *I John 1:5*

> *"...you are a chosen generation, a royal priesthood, a holy nation, His own special people, that you may proclaim the praises of **Him who called you out of darkness into His marvelous light**..." **I Peter 2:9***

> *"...He (God) has **delivered us from the power of darkness** and conveyed us into the kingdom of the Son of His love..." **Colossians 1:13***

> *"...Put on the whole armor of God, that you may be able to stand against the wiles of the devil. For we do not wrestle against flesh and blood, but against principalities, against powers, against the **rulers of the darkness of this age**, against spiritual hosts of wickedness in heavenly places..." **Ephesians 6:10-12***

> *"...Saul, Saul, why are you persecuting Me? It is hard for you to kick against the goads. So I said, 'Who are You, Lord?' And He said, 'I am Jesus, whom you are persecuting. But rise and stand on your feet; for I have appeared to you for this purpose, to make you a minister and a witness both of the things which you have seen and of the things which I will yet reveal to you. I will deliver you from the Jewish people, as well as from the Gentiles, to whom I now send you, to open their eyes, in order to **turn them from darkness to light, and from the power of Satan to God**, that they may receive forgiveness of sins and an inheritance among those who are sanctified by faith in Me." **Acts 26:14-18***

The Lamb's Blood

Adam's enslavement *"...to sin leading to death..."* made Satan, *"...him who had the power of death..."* and ruler *"...of the darkness of this age..."*, Adam's master. We have already seen in Scripture *"...through one man sin entered the world, and death through sin, and thus death spread to all men..."*. Satan in affect became the *"...god of this age..." (**II Corinthians 4:4**)* or in Jesus' words *"...the ruler of this world..." (**John 12:31** [compare: **Matthew 4:1-11** esp vs **8,9**])*.

God's kingdom is the antithesis of Satan's kingdom. God desires to *"...deliver us from the power of darkness..."*, from Satan's rule, and to convey us *"...into the kingdom of the Son of His love..." (**Colossians 1:13**)*. God sent His Son into the world *"...that the world through Him might be saved..." (**John 3:17**)*. **Jesus came to *"...redeem..."* us!** While Jesus was in the world He provided healing for all who would receive it. Matthew wrote about Jesus taking our infirmities and bearing our sicknesses as fulfillment of a prophesy given by Isaiah.

> *"When evening had come, they brought to Him many who were demon-possessed. And He cast out the spirits with a word, and healed all who were sick, that it might be fulfilled which was spoken by Isaiah the prophet, saying,*
>
> > *'He Himself took our infirmities and bore our sicknesses.'*
> > *(original prophesy found in **Isaiah 53:4,5**)*
> > ***Matthew 8:16,17***

Is "...healing..." included then in our redemption?

Lord of Healing

In *Chapter Eight* of my last book **Birthed into the Supernatural** redemption was an important topic. The considerations of redemption in *Chapter Eight* do not specifically answer the question whether healing is a part of our redemption, but they help move us forward toward finding an answer.

> "The redemption we obtained through Jesus Christ is an *"...eternal redemption..." (Hebrews 9:12)*. That is, Jesus' sacrifice as *"...the Lamb of God to take away the sin of the world..." (John 1:29)* will last forever! The *"...blood of bulls and goats and the ashes of a heifer..." (Hebrews 9:13)* used as sacrifices for sin in the old covenant are temporal and have to be sacrificed year after year *(Hebrews 10:1)*. Jesus needed to die only once. His blood is eternally alive, cleansing us from all sin, providing eternal redemption for all.
>
> Because the redemption Christ provides is an *"...eternal redemption..." (Hebrews 9:12)*, it is greater than anything temporal. The laws of the natural temporal universe do not apply to anything eternal. Past, present, and future are all temporal terms. Jesus' death, burial, and resurrection are eternal. That is why Jesus does not have to die over and over again every time anyone calls on Him for salvation. The *"...eternal redemption..." (Hebrews 9:12)* He provided is for all mankind for all generations for all time. All man has to do is appropriate what already exists!"

We understand it is by Jesus' blood *(Hebrews 9:12)*, shed at the time of His death, that our eternal redemption was wrought. But how does healing fit into this redemption? Throughout the New Testament Jesus repeatedly testified He came only to do the will of His Father *(John 4:34; Hebrews 10:9; John 5:30; Matthew 26:39; Luke 22;42)* .

> *"...For I have come down from heaven, not to do My own will, but the will of Him who sent Me...."*
> **John 6:38**

Every *"...work..."* Jesus did was the will of His Father! Jesus actually told His disciples *"...the Father who dwells in Me does the works..." **(John 14:10)**.*

On a certain Sabbath Jesus went into the synagogue and read from the book of the prophet Isaiah. What He read provided a summary statement for the *"...works..."* of His ministry.

> *"So He (Jesus) came to Nazareth, where He had been brought up. And as His custom was, He went into the synagogue on the Sabbath day, and stood up to read. And He was handed the book of the prophet Isaiah. And when He had opened the book, He found the place where it was written:*
>
> > *'The Spirit of the Lord is upon Me, because He has anointed Me to preach the gospel to the poor; He has sent Me to heal the brokenhearted, to proclaim liberty to the captives and recovery of sight to the blind, to set at liberty those who are oppressed; to proclaim the acceptable year of the Lord.'*
>
> *Then He closed the book, and gave it back to the attendant and sat down. And the eyes of all who were in the synagogue were fixed on Him. And He began to say to them, 'Today this Scripture is fulfilled in your hearing."*
> **Luke 4:16-21**

Luke was inspired to write here that *"...healing..."* in one form or another was included in the *"...works..."* of Jesus' earthly ministry. Luke recorded Jesus saying the Spirit of the Lord anointed Him to do the works He did. All of the works of Jesus' earthly ministry were a prelude leading to His work of redemption to be accomplished ultimately through His death.

Healing was a significant part of Jesus' ministry while He was on earth. Using another reference from *Chapter Eight* of my last book, **Birthed into the Supernatural**, we revisit the basis for our redemption.

> "Jesus came into the world as *"...the Lamb of God to take away the sin of the world..." (**John 1:29**)*. He accomplished this by living a sinless life so He could be the sacrifice to take away our sins *(**II Corinthians 5:21; I Peter 1:18-21**)*. He died on the cross as the ultimate sacrifice, carrying our sins in Himself, allowing His own blood to be shed for us *(**I Peter 2:23-25**)*. Jesus' death, burial, and resurrection provide salvation for all mankind."

Peter wrote in his first epistle *"...by whose (Jesus') stripes you were healed..."*. This declaration specifically includes *"...healing..."* in the same context discussing Jesus *"...bearing our sins in His own body..."*, which we typically accept as the core of our *"...eternal redemption..."*.

> *"...(Jesus) Himself bore our sins in His own body on the tree, that we, having died to sins, might live for righteousness -- by whose stripes you were healed..."*
> **I Peter 2:24**

There is no conclusive evidence in this verse, nor the context of which it is a part, definitively determining the part of man to which the *"...healing..."* specifically applies *(...his spirit, his soul, or his body...)*. However, it is clear throughout the entire New Testament Jesus' earthly ministry included healing people's bodies of physical infirmities as the will of God *(Matthew 8:16,17; Matthew 9:20-22, 35; Luke 17:11-19; Mark 10:46-52)*. Combined from all four gospels, there are at least 81 separate accounts of Jesus healing people. Healing sickness and disease was part of Jesus' ministry, who came only to do the will of His Father. The Father's purpose in sending Jesus into the world included His *"...taking our infirmities and bearing our sicknesses..."* *(Matthew 8:17)*.

We know our God to be a Triune God comprised of three separable and identifiable parts yet One True God: God the Father, God the Son, and God the Holy Spirit. Scripture teaches all three parts of the Trinity were directly involved in healing men's bodies. Jesus said the Spirit of the Lord anointed Him to do the works of His ministry *(Luke 4:16-21)*. He also said it was the Father dwelling in Him who did the works *(John 14:9-11)*.

Consider the topic of *"...deliverance..."* to help us gain an important understanding. When Jesus cast a demon out of a certain individual among the multitudes, some marveled, others said, *"...He casts out demons by Beelzebub, the ruler of the demons..."(Luke 11:15)*. Beelzebub is another name commonly accepted for Satan. Surely no Christian believes Jesus was in league with Satan as the means of casting out demons. Jesus made it clear He cast out demons *"...with the finger of God..."* *(Luke 11:20)*, not by Beelzebub. Because demons are members of the satanic kingdom, Satan could not be the source of deliverance from demons or his kingdom would be divided against itself, as Jesus explained in the following Scripture recorded by Luke.

> *"And He (Jesus) was casting out a demon, and it was mute. So it was, when the demon had gone out, that the mute spoke; and the multitudes marveled. But some of them said, 'He casts out demons by Beelzebub, the ruler of the demons.' Others, testing Him, sought from Him a sign from heaven. But He, knowing their thoughts, said to them: **'Every kingdom divided against itself is brought to desolation, and a house divided against a house falls. If Satan also is divided against himself, how will his kingdom stand?...'"***
> **Luke 11:14-23 & Matthew 12:23-30**

If infirmity, sickness, and disease are parts of God's kingdom and any or all three parts of the Trinity were involved in healing man of sickness and disease, then God's kingdom would be divided in exactly the same manner Jesus described in **Luke 11:14-23**. Sickness and disease simply cannot be parts of the kingdom of God.

As we have already seen in Scripture, the Holy Spirit inspired God's kingdom of light to be contrasted with the kingdom of darkness ruled by Satan *(I John 1:5; I Peter 2:9; Colossians 1:13; Ephesians 6:10-12)*. Paul was sent to the Gentiles to *"...turn them from darkness to light, and from the power of Satan to God..." (Acts 26:14-18)*.

Infirmity, sickness, and disease, which simply cannot be parts of God's kingdom, can, alternatively, be identified with the kingdom of darkness, the place where Satan rules. Infirmity, sickness, and disease certainly conform to the three characteristics with which Jesus described the thief who *"...does not come except to steal, and to kill, and to destroy...."* ***(John 10:10)***. In contrast, Jesus said of Himself, *"...I have come that they may have life, and that they may have it more abundantly..."* ***(John 10:10)***. Whether infirmity, sickness, and disease are directly from Satan or not, they do not promote abundance of life; more accurately they *"...steal, kill, and destroy..."* just like the thief. We know infirmity, sickness, and disease can be pathways leading to death. Anything which steals, kills, destroys, or can lead to death can easily be called a power which comes out of darkness. When we were born again Abba *"...delivered us from the power of darkness and conveyed us into the kingdom of the Son of His love..."* ***(Colossians 1:13)***.

A simple definition for *"...disease..."* is illusive. However, the majority of sources attempting to define disease included this or similar terminology *"...a harmful deviation from normal..."*. Infirmity, sickness, and disease infringe on the *"...normal..."* human condition. Whenever anyone becomes sick or diseased, they will go to extraordinary lengths to find relief. Everyone who has ever been sick recognizes infirmity, sickness, and disease as unwanted and unacceptable parts of their natural life.

Our conveyance into the *"...kingdom of the Son of His love..."* is very specific. Although Scripture refers to our baptism into Christ as a *"...great mystery..."*, nevertheless, the Holy Spirit inspired Paul to write...

Lord of Healing

> *"...we are members of His body, of His flesh and of His bones. For this reason a man shall leave his father and mother and be joined to his wife, and the two shall become one flesh. This is a great mystery, but I speak concerning Christ and the church..."* **Ephesians 5:30-32**

Our *"...flesh and bone..."* membership in Christ's body has great bearing on the manner of life we are to live. Consider the issue of sexual immorality Paul addressed regarding *"...members of Christ's body..."* in his letter to the church at Corinth. What he was inspired to write is poignant and very profound. The actions of the members of Christ's body directly affect Christ.

> *"...Do you not know that your bodies are members of Christ? Shall I then take the members of Christ and make them members of a harlot? Certainly not!..."* **I Corinthians 6:15**

As we have already seen infirmity, sickness, and disease simply cannot be parts of God's kingdom, then how could they be acceptable parts of the *"...flesh and bone..."* members of Christ's body? Any acceptable attachment of them to the *"...flesh and bone..."* members of Christ's body would make them acceptable parts of Christ in exactly the same manner as Paul described in *I Corinthians 6:15*. *God forbid!*

Scripture is clear Jesus' blood is the means by which *"...eternal redemption..."* was wrought *(Hebrews 9:12)*. Every drop of the *"...Lamb's..."* blood shed at the time of His death, whether produced by the stripes on His back from the cruel Roman whip, the violent beatings He was made to endure, the crown of thorns placed on His head, the nails driven in His hands and feet, or the spear thrust into His side, every drop of it was the *"...blood..."* necessary to secure our *"...eternal redemption..."*!

The Lamb's Blood

Because infirmity, sickness, and disease are not parts of God's kingdom and because they steal, kill, and destroy, they are something from which we need to be freed. The blood Jesus shed at the time of His death is the means of providing us everything we need to be free. The Father accepted Jesus' blood as the means of freeing all mankind for all generations for all time. This freedom, called the *"...eternal redemption..."*, is the foundation of the new covenant.

The new covenant offers man a divinely empowered means of being freed from the power of darkness and living abundant eternal lives.

> *"...For by grace you have been saved through faith, and that not of yourselves; it is the gift of God, not of works, lest anyone should boast..."* **(Ephesians 2:8,9)**.

By *"...faith..."* we appropriate salvation, forgiveness, deliverance, and *"...healing..."!* All of these things are provisions of the new covenant which flow out of the *"...eternal redemption..."* established by the precious blood of the Lamb!

We must keep the revelation of *"...healing..."* accurate and simple in order to escape the traditions and doctrine of man by which we have lived too long. Jesus came into the world to *"...save..."* us from every corruption that does not conform to the will and way of God. Jesus said of Himself, *"...I am the way, the truth, and the life..." (John 14:6)*. Jesus is to be the *"...way..."* we live. Infirmity, sickness, and disease are not the way of Christ. Remember these three things...

Lord of Healing

If God heals anyone of infirmity, sickness, and disease, then they cannot be a part of God or His kingdom otherwise He would be divided in exactly the same manner Jesus described in ***Luke 11:14-23***.

Although Jesus divested Himself of His divine attributes to live as a man, He is still part of the Triune God! Because infirmity, sickness, and disease cannot be parts of God or His kingdom, they cannot be a part of Christ.

Any acceptable attachment of infirmity, sickness, and disease to the *"...flesh and bone..."* members of Christ's body would make them acceptable parts of Christ in exactly the same manner as Paul described in ***I Corinthians 6:15***. That is unacceptable.

It is God's will that we be healed from infirmity, sickness, and disease. Jesus' shed blood provided opportunity for us to be free from them. The means of appropriating this freedom is faith, a gift from God!

Chapter Two
Why?

If healing is the will of God then why are so many sick? The answer is linked to a powerful understanding everyone must gain regarding the will of God. In this dispensation man has freedom to choose God's will or not, based on their knowledge of His will! Whatever God wills must be revealed as His will, received as His will, accepted and walked out as a conscious choice of the heart from each person on an individual basis.

Consider *"...salvation..."* as one such illustration. Paul wrote by inspiration of the Holy Spirit revealing the will of God for *"...all men to be saved..."*.

> *"Therefore I exhort first of all that supplications, prayers, intercessions, and giving of thanks be made for all men, for kings and all who are in authority, that we may lead a quiet and peaceable life in all godliness and reverence. For this is good and acceptable in the sight of* **God our Savior, who desires (2309 [*...wills... (2309) KJV])* all men to be saved and to come to the knowledge of the truth...*" I Timothy 2:1-4*

2309 thelo -- desire, be disposed (forward), intent, list, love, mean, please, have rather, (be) will (have, -ling, -ling [ly]).

Strong's Exhaustive Concordance of the Bible

Lord of Healing

The Greek term *thelo* in *I Timothy 2:4* is translated *desires* in the *NKJV* and *wills* in the *KJV*. **Strong's Concordance** includes in its definition of *thelo* both *desire* and *will*. In other words, whenever the Greek term *thelo* is used it can be translated into English using either *desire* or *will*. This has particular significance when applied to God, especially in *I Timothy 2:4*. God's *desire* for *"...all men to be saved..."* is His *will!*

> ***Whatever God desires is also what He wills!***

In His conversation with Nicodemus Jesus presented the source of *"...salvation..."* for all men.

> *"For God so loved the world that He gave His only begotten Son, that whoever believes in Him should not perish but have everlasting life. For God did not send His Son into the world to condemn the world, but that the world through Him might be saved."* **John 3:16,17**

And finally, Paul wrote in his letter to the church at Rome about how man could appropriate this wonderful *"...salvation..."*.

> *"...whoever calls on the name of the Lord shall be saved. How then shall they call on Him in whom they have not believed? And how shall they believe in Him of whom they have not heard? And how shall they hear without a preacher? And how shall they preach unless they are sent?"* **Romans 10:13,14**

God wills for *"...all men to be saved..."*. He *"...gave His only begotten Son..."* as an act of His will to be the source of our

Why?

"...salvation...". And *"...whoever calls on the name of the Lord shall be saved...".* However, look at the sequence presented in **Romans 10:13,14** required for a person to be able to call on Jesus as the source of their salvation. The person must believe. They believe as a result of hearing. They hear because someone preached to them. Someone preached because they were sent to do so.

This Scriptural pattern, written by Paul and inspired by God the Holy Spirit, in **Romans 10:13,14** does not exclude the possibility of a person calling on Jesus without someone preaching to them. The pattern is not the only way a person can learn of Jesus. Instead, the pattern presents the prerequisites leading up to salvation, whether involving another person who has been sent to tell us about Jesus or our own independent search. The prerequisites are principally the same. We cannot call on Jesus in order to be saved without having first learned of Him and believed on Him.

God's will for a person to be saved **"...does not operate automatically...".** There are prerequisites leading up to a person being able to appropriate salvation. Understanding the concept of prerequisites is pivotal to our being able to appropriate the provisions of the new covenant.

In the same manner as in salvation, it is the will of God for us to be healed of sickness and disease. However, His will for us to be healed **"...does not operate automatically...".** There are prerequisites leading up to our being able to appropriate healing. We must believe healing is the will of God. We will only be able to do this if we have sound doctrine regarding healing. We will only have such doctrine if someone teaches us or if we have received it directly from the Holy Spirit through our own search. And we must believe what we have received, whether from our own search or from what someone taught us. This is the same pattern of which Paul wrote regarding salvation *(Romans 10:13-17)*.

Doctrine plays an amazing role in our Christian lives in what we learn of and how we relate to Christ. Paul wrote about doctrine in his second letter to Timothy linking it to Scripture.

> *"All Scripture is given by inspiration of God, and is profitable for doctrine, for reproof, for correction, for instruction in righteousness, that the man of God may be complete, thoroughly equipped for every good work."*
> ***II Timothy 3:16,17***

Doctrine, which gains its profitability from Scripture, is one of the components designed to help *"...the man of God be complete, thoroughly equipped for every good work...".*

An over simplified definition of doctrine is *"...teaching...".* Our doctrine either leads us to Christ or away from Him. Sound doctrine leads us directly to Christ so we may start the process of appropriating the provisions of the new covenant. Unsound doctrine leads us directly toward tradition and the doctrine of man aborting the provisions of the covenant and making the power of God ineffective in our lives *(Compare **Matthew 15:1-11** & **Mark 7:1-13**).*

Why?

Many people are born again and immediately begin to be *"...indoctrinated..."* with teaching that does not lead them to Christ. Even though they may have truly been born again, the way they live never seems to change. A person may not change the way they live as a result of a rebellious heart. However, the notion that a person can accept Jesus the Lord as the means of being born again but continue to live life not submitted to Jesus as Lord is too often a result of what the person has been taught.

Consider what God the Holy Spirit inspired James to write regarding *"...Lordship..."*.

> *"Come now, you who say, 'Today or tomorrow we will go to such and such a city, spend a year there, buy and sell, and make a profit'; whereas you do not know what will happen tomorrow. For what is your life? It is even a vapor that appears for a little time and then vanishes away. Instead you ought to say, 'If the Lord wills, we shall live and do this or that.' But now you boast in your arrogance. All such boasting is evil."*
> **James 4:13-16**

James was writing to the church. He was writing to born again people who evidently were not living their daily lives submitted to Jesus as Lord. The people to whom James wrote were not the only Scriptural illustration of born again people not submitting to Jesus as Lord of their daily lives. The church at Laodicea whom Jesus rebuked represents another such illustration **(Revelation 3:14-22)**.

Sound doctrine teaches submission to the Lordship of Christ opens the door to the benefits which come from the authority Jesus has been given to be Lord over us. Jesus desires for us to have the abundance of life which is only available by making Him *"...Lord..."* of our daily lives. He does not desire to *"...subjugate..."* us and control our lives. He wants us to yield gladly of our own free will. When we see the great benefit of yielding to Him, we will.

> *"Without faith it is impossible to please Him, for he who comes to God must believe that He is, and that He is a rewarder of those who diligently seek Him."*
> **Hebrews 11:6**

Sound doctrine is a necessity for living successfully in the church! It seems as if there are as many *"...doctrines..."* about *"..healing..."* as there are people in the church. Surely, we can see the devices of the enemy at work in this inconsistency. He comes with all subtly to deceive us into accepting his corruption so he can *"...steal..."* the provisions of the kingdom from us. He is truly a thief, just as Jesus said!

However, Jesus has commissioned persons called to offices of ministry to receive revelation necessary for us to appropriate all He died to provide. Jesus also asked the Father to give us the Holy Spirit. Through the Holy Spirit we are able to receive the revelation of Christ and are enabled to freely give what we have freely received. It is the will of God for us to have sound doctrine regarding healing *and* the healing such doctrine reveals.

Why?

Embedded within our salvation experience is a profound understanding absolutely necessary for us to be able to live healthy lives after our new birth. Although a person may have been seeking only salvation and not relationship at the time of their new birth, the means to salvation is relationship with Jesus as Lord. Any effort to live a saved life without continual daily relationship with Jesus will end in failure! Paul wrote to the church at Philippi *"...work out your own salvation with fear and trembling..." **(Philippians 2:12)**.*

Jesus said, *"...this is life eternal, that they may know You, the only true God, and Jesus Christ whom You have sent..." **(John 17:3)**.* In His conversation with Nicodemus, Jesus contrasted perishing with eternal and everlasting life.

> *"...And as Moses lifted up the serpent in the wilderness, even so must the Son of Man be lifted up, that whoever believes in Him should not perish but have eternal life. For God so loved the world that He gave His only begotten Son, that whoever believes in Him should not perish but have everlasting life. For God did not send His Son into the world to condemn the world, but that the world through Him might be saved...."*
> **John 3:14-17**

Jesus said *"...life eternal..."* is *"...knowing God..." **(John 17:3)**.* It is the knowledge we receive of Jesus that gives us opportunity to enter into relationship with Him as Lord. This relationship ushers us into eternal and everlasting life!

Scripture makes it frighteningly clear there is an enormous difference between knowing *"...about..."* God and

Lord of Healing

"...knowing..." God as the way we live. Knowing about God does not correctly cause a person to change the way they live. Perhaps the most dramatic illustration of this truth comes through the words Jesus spoke to lawless people as recorded by Matthew.

> *"Not everyone who says to Me, 'Lord, Lord,' shall enter the kingdom of heaven, but he who does the will of My Father in heaven. Many will say to Me in that day, 'Lord, Lord, have we not prophesied in Your name, cast out demons in Your name, and done many wonders in Your name?' And then I will declare to them, 'I never knew you: depart from Me, you who practice lawlessness!'*
> **Matthew 7:21-23**

Every provision of the new covenant is inextricably linked with Jesus! Anyone who calls on Him will be saved, but Scripture makes it clear a person cannot call on Him of whom they have not heard and believed. If a person desires to be saved, they must know Jesus as Lord. This knowledge of Jesus is not merely knowing about Him as Lord; it is entering into relationship with Him as Lord. This relationship will correctly inspire us to change the way we live our daily lives. However, as we have already seen in James' letter to born again people who were not living submitted to Jesus on a daily basis *(James 4:13-17)*, people do not always yield to correct inspiration to change the way they live after new birth. The lack of change can come from a rebellious heart, lack of sound doctrine, or unsound doctrine.

Christ Jesus the Lord is the source of all we seek! Every provision of the new covenant is designed to be based on

Why?

our relationship with Jesus. If a person desires to be healed, they must know Christ as Healer. We can obtain sound doctrine in this matter by searching for it on our own or by learning it from someone who has come to teach us. Either way, we must have accurate knowledge of Christ in order to appropriate the healing He came to provide.

The letter Paul wrote to the Colossian church reveals the intent of our God regarding our redemption.

> *"...He (God) has delivered us from the power of darkness and conveyed us into the kingdom of the Son of His love..."* **Colossians 1:13** *(See context verses 9-23)*

The plan of salvation was not only to deliver us from the power of darkness but also to convey us into the kingdom of the Son of His love. God planned for Jesus to take care of us after we were birthed into His kingdom. Jesus' Lordship is intended for so much more than our just being born again. It is to be the way we live on a daily basis involving every area of our lives including healing.

Unsound doctrine teaches us to seek the provisions of the kingdom as our priority: *"Seek the things the Gentiles seek!"* If this device does not deceive us, the enemy launches the opposite extreme: *"All things the Gentiles seek are ungodly and to be avoided!"* Both of these are devices of the enemy set in place to *"...steal..."* what is rightfully ours. Jesus did not say ***never*** to seek the things the Gentiles seek. He said to seek *"...**first** the kingdom of God and His righteousness, and all* *these things shall be added to you..." **(Matthew 6:33)**.* Jesus is the source of all we seek. If we seek Him, we will find what we desire! *...including the things the Gentiles seek **and** healing for our bodies!*

Chapter Three
Appropriating Healing

Jesus is *"...the way, the truth, and the life..."* we are to live! As we have already seen, if infirmity, sickness, and disease are parts of God's kingdom and any part of the Trinity was involved in healing man of them, then God and His kingdom would be divided in exactly the same manner Jesus described in **Luke 11:14-23**. Infirmity, sickness, and disease simply cannot be parts of God nor His kingdom. And we have also already seen any acceptable attachment of infirmity, sickness, and disease to the *"...flesh and bone..."* members of Christ's body would make them acceptable parts of Christ in exactly the same manner as Paul described in **I Corinthians 6:15**. Infirmity, sickness, and disease are not to be acceptable parts of our lives!

Jesus gave us a description of the thief and immediately followed with a comparative description of Himself.

> *"The thief does not come except to steal, and to kill, and to destroy. I have come that they (His sheep) may have life, and that they may have it more abundantly."*
> **John 10:10**

Because we live in this world where Satan is ruler *(John 12:31),* we will encounter many of his devices intended *"...to steal, to kill, and to destroy...".* Whenever we encounter infirmity, sickness or disease, if we have sound doctrine, we know they simply cannot be parts of the Triune God nor His kingdom. We will then resist them just as we are to resist the devil *(Compare James 4:7).*

Hopefully, we are persuaded *"...sin..."* is not of God! Yet persons who are born again children of God can and do sin. If a born again person is tempted and sins, we do not blame the person's choice nor the temptation on God because we know sin is not of God. Instead, we repent of our sin, receive forgiveness, and go forward free of the sin. Consider what James was inspired to write in this matter.

> *"Let no one say when he is tempted, 'I am tempted by God'; for God cannot be tempted by evil, nor does He Himself tempt anyone. But each one is tempted when he is drawn away by his own desires and enticed. Then, when desire has conceived, it gives birth to sin; and sin, when it is full-grown, brings forth death. Do not be deceived, my beloved brethren. Every good gift and every perfect gift is from above, and comes down from the Father of lights, with whom there is no variation or shadow of turning."* ***James 1:13-17***

Forgiveness of sin is the will of God *(I John 1:9)* just as salvation is the will of God *(John 3:16,17)*. Because the new covenant is a faith covenant, every facet of it is to be walked out in faith. *"For we walk by faith, not by sight."* ***II Corinthians 5:7***. Whether we desire to appropriate forgiveness, or salvation, or some other provision of the new covenant, we do so by faith according to our knowledge of the will of God.

The new covenant and all of its provisions are established on the foundation of the eternal redemption wrought by the shed blood of Christ *(Hebrews 9:12)*. It is important to note however, that *"...mercy..."* is not a provision of the **new covenant**. It is an eternal characteristic of the Most High God made available *"...new every morning..."* *(**Lamentations 3:22,23**)*. In

Appropriating Healing

Matthew's account of Peter walking on water he records, *"...when he saw that the wind was boisterous, he was afraid; and beginning to sink he cried out, saying, 'Lord, save me!'..." (Matthew 14:22-33)*. Clearly we see Peter desired to be *"...saved..."*, but he was not asking for *"...eternal and everlasting life..."*. He knew his faith was failing in his water-walking-experience so he was asking for *"...mercy..."*. Even though Jesus rebuked Peter saying, *"...O you of little faith, why did you doubt?..."*, I am confident Peter was delighted to have received the mercies of God extended through Christ.

Whenever a person desires to be *"...saved..."*, appropriate eternal and everlasting life as provisions of the new covenant, Jesus is not required to shed His blood over and over again to fulfill every person's desire *(Hebrews 9:23-28)*. It was necessary for Jesus to shed His blood only once to provide salvation for all mankind for all time. Salvation has been deposited into a heavenly account and is available to *"...whoever calls on the name of the Lord..."* to appropriate it by faith. So, too, healing has been deposited into a heavenly account and is available to whoever has sound doctrine in the matter and whoever will exercise faith to appropriate it.

The means of appropriating salvation is by confessing Jesus as Lord. As we have already seen the prerequisites necessary to be able to call on Jesus are simple and clear. A person must believe on Jesus as a result of having heard of Him through someone preaching to them because they were sent to do so. A person must have sound doctrine regarding Christ in order to have faith to call on Him to be saved. A person's confession of Jesus as Lord causes them to enter into relationship with Him which in turn ushers them into eternal and everlasting life!

Consider John's testimony of Jesus' earthly ministry.

> *"...He (Jesus) came to His own, and His own did not receive Him. But as many as received Him, to them He gave the right to become children of God, to those who believe in His name; who were born, not of blood, nor of the will of the flesh, nor of the will of man, but of God."* **John 1:11-13**

The priority in John's testimony is people receiving *"...Jesus..."* as a result of the knowledge they had received of Him! The knowledge they had of Him is what caused them to be able to enter into relationship with Him. The ensuing relationship is what caused them to be born again as children of God!

As we have already stated, *"It seems as if there are as many "...doctrines..." about "..healing..." as there are people in the church."*. We do not blame God for the temptation with which people are tempted nor for our choice to sin because we know sin is not of God *(James 1:13-17)*. In exactly the same way, we must not blame God for infirmity, sickness, and disease because we know they cannot possibly be of God! As we move toward understanding how to appropriate healing, we must believe that healing is God's will.

Without trying to create a new statement different from what we have already written, we will simply quote from *Chapter One, pages 10 and 11,* how *"...healing..."* is the will of God.

Appropriating Healing

Scripture is clear Jesus' blood is the means by which *"...eternal redemption..."* was wrought *(Hebrews 9:12)*. Every drop of the *"...Lamb's..."* blood shed at the time of His death, whether produced by the stripes on His back from the cruel Roman whip, the violent beatings He was made to endure, the crown of thorns placed on His head, the nails driven in His hands and feet, or the spear thrust into His side, all of it is the *"...blood..."* necessary to secure our *"...eternal redemption..."*!

Because infirmity, sickness, and disease are not parts of God's kingdom and because they steal, kill, and destroy, they are something from which we need to be freed. The blood Jesus shed at the time of His death is the means of providing us everything we need to be free. The Father accepted Jesus' blood as the means of freeing all mankind for all generations for all time. This freedom, called the *"...eternal redemption..."*, is the foundation of the new covenant.

Understanding that *"...healing..."* is something Christ's shed blood has already provided, not something He needs to provide over and over again, is essential for us to be able to appropriate healing according to God's will. Perhaps a natural world illustration would make it easier to understand this principle.

Consider a college student asking his parents for financial help. His parents were zealous and able to help, so they told him they would deposit a certain amount of money into the bank on his behalf. They deposited the money and told him they had done so. The next day their son called again asking for money. The parents asked their son what he had done with the money they deposited on his behalf yesterday. But the son continued to insist he needed money. His parents thought something must be wrong. They were concerned the deposit may not have arrived at the bank. Or perhaps the bank had not posted the deposit. They asked their son if he had tried to cash a check for the amount they deposited on his behalf. He replied he had not.

A foolish illustration? Maybe, however, it demonstrates how the very thing the student desired had already been deposited into the bank on his behalf, yet he still did not have the *"...money..."* the deposit represented. The son only needed to believe his parents had deposited the money, write a check for the amount of the deposit, and he could have had what he desired. Continuing to ask his parents for money when they had already deposited money into the bank on his behalf greatly hindered the process of his appropriating the money he desired.

If you need healing, you must have sound doctrine regarding the will of God concerning healing. Healing, like salvation, is paid for by Jesus' shed blood. Healing, like salvation, has been deposited into a heavenly account and is available to whoever will appropriate it by faith. To ask God continually to heal you is so very similar to the college student continually asking his parents for money when in fact money had already been deposited into the bank on his behalf.

Appropriating Healing

Jesus paid the price for our redemption! All of the provisions of the new covenant have already been deposited into the heavenly account for all mankind for all time. Jesus provided an *"...eternal redemption..."* not bound or controlled by the temporal in any way! Desire to understand the things of God related to our eternal redemption is a holy and noble desire. As long as we keep before us our natural man cannot study enough, have a high enough IQ, or desire enough to cause God to change the way of the new covenant. The old covenant was based on man's ability to understand and to do. The new covenant is based on the ability God gives us to understand and to do. Understanding the things of God related to our eternal redemption can only be done if God reveals them *(I Corinthians 2:9-14)* and if we receive them by faith with our spirit.

Isaiah prophesied about the coming Messiah. His words are a summary of the ministry Messiah would provide. The entire chapter *Isaiah 53:1-12* speaks of the coming Savior.

> *"Who has believed our report? And to whom has the arm of the Lord been revealed? For He shall grow up before Him as a tender plant, and as a root out of dry ground. He has no form or comeliness; and when we see Him, there is no beauty that we should desire Him. He is despised and rejected by men, a man of sorrows and acquainted with grief. And we hid, as it were, our faces from Him; He was despised and we did not esteem Him. Surely He has borne our griefs and carried our sorrows; yet we esteemed Him stricken, smitten by God, and afflicted. But He was wounded for our transgressions, He was bruised for our iniquities; the chastisement for our peace was upon Him, and by His stripes we are healed. All we like sheep have gone astray; we have turned, every one, to his own way; and the Lord has laid*

Lord of Healing

on Him the iniquity of us all. He was oppressed and He was afflicted, yet He opened not His mouth; He was led as a lamb to the slaughter, and as a sheep before its shearers is silent, so He opened not His mouth. He was taken from prison and from judgment, and who will declare His generation? For He was cut off from the land of the living; for the transgressions of My people He was stricken. And they made His grave with the wicked -- but with the rich at His death, because He had done no violence, nor was any deceit in His mouth. Yet it pleased the Lord to bruise Him; He has put Him to grief. When You make His soul an offering for sin, He shall see His seed, He shall prolong His days, and the pleasure of the Lord shall prosper in His hand. He shall see the labor of His soul, and be satisfied. By His knowledge My righteous Servant shall justify many, for He shall bear their iniquities. Therefore I will divide Him a portion with the great, and He shall divide the spoil with the strong, because He poured out His soul unto death, and was numbered with the transgressors, and He bore the sin of many, and made intercession for the transgressors."
Isaiah 53:1-12

Isaiah's prophecy provides a beautiful but dreadful description of the earthly ministry of Jesus. Scripture makes it very clear it was Jesus' shed blood and His death which provided the *"...eternal redemption..."* **(Hebrews 9:11-15)**. However, there were many prerequisites required to get Jesus into position to be able to shed His blood and to die on the cross. Beginning with the immaculate conception and including every event prior to His final breath on the tree, they were all parts of His life and ministry required leading up to the consummation of the *"...eternal redemption..."*. Absolutely everything about *"...the word being made flesh..."* was expressing the love of God to redeem us.

Appropriating Healing

Every breath Jesus took on earth was a breath He took to redeem us. All that we seek comes out of relationship with God. Appropriating the provisions of the new covenant is not meant to become a clinical legalistic process. It is not about saying the right words in the right order the right way. It is about knowing God!

The Word of God, the second part of the Trinity, was willing to divest Himself of His divine attributes and come to the earth clothed in flesh as a man. He was willing to endure the tedious process of His mother's pregnancy and even be birthed in a manger. He was willing to live as a man facing all the conditions that every other man faced *(except of course Adam's sin)*. Even in His prayerful preparation for His crucifixion, sweating great drops of blood in Gethsemane *(Luke 22:40-46)*, Scripture says, *"...for the joy that was set before Him endured the cross..." (Hebrews 12:2)*. Even in His agony, Jesus was thinking about us and our redemption. Redeeming us brought joy to Him.

The words of Jesus' prayer to His Father are so much more meaningful when considering them from the perspective of relationship. *"This is eternal life, that they may know You, the only true God, and Jesus Christ whom You have sent"* **John 17:3**. If we desire to be saved, we must draw near to Jesus with our hearts full of thanksgiving for His willingness to do all it took to make a way for us to live and not die. With that understanding in our hearts, we tell Jesus we receive Him and desire to make Him the Lord of our life. The moment we take these personal and intimate steps of relationship with the Christ, we

Lord of Healing

are granted *"...the right to become children of God..." **(John 1:12)***. Everything we seek comes out of relationship with Christ!

If we desire healing, we must draw near to Jesus with our hearts full of thanksgiving for His willingness to have provided healing for us; thanksgiving for His willingness to *"...take our infirmities and bear our sicknesses..."*; thanksgiving for His willingness to allow His blood to be shed in death as the price of our healing, part of our eternal redemption. With this understanding in our hearts, we tell Jesus we receive Him as Healer. Now we can begin to resist infirmities, sicknesses and diseases as part of the preparation necessary to appropriate our healing.

If we accept Christ as our Healer, then how does infirmity, sickness, or disease access our bodies? That is an excellent question! The simplest most direct answer is, *They trespass!* Jesus' shed blood purchased us. Paul exhorted the elders from Ephesus to...

> *"...take heed to yourselves and to the flock, among which the Holy Spirit has made you overseers, to shepherd the church of God which He purchased with His own blood..."* **Acts 20:28**

In addressing the issue of sexual immorality in the church at Corinth, Paul wrote one of the most powerful statements in the entire New Testament about our bodies as members of Christ and the impact we have on Christ as such.

> *"Do you not know that your bodies are members of Christ? Shall I then take the members of Christ and*

Appropriating Healing

> *make them members of a harlot? Certainly not! Or do you now know that he who is joined to a harlot is one body with her? For 'the two', He says, 'shall become one flesh.' But he who is joined to the Lord is one spirit with Him. Flee sexual immorality. Every sin that a man does is outside the body, but he who commits sexual immorality sins against his own body. Or do you not know that your body is the temple of the Holy Spirit who is in you, whom you have from God, and you are not your own? For you were bought at a price; therefore glorify God in your body and in your spirit, which are God's..."*
> **I Corinthians 6:19-20**

Repeatedly in the New Testament born again believers are identified as *"...the body of Christ..."* **(Romans 6:3; 12:5; I Corinthians 1:17; Galatians 3:15-29; Ephesians 1:22,23)**. What Paul wrote comparing marriage with Christ and the church is particularly important in this matter.

> *"...no one ever hated his own flesh, but nourishes and cherishes it, just as the Lord does the church. For we are members of His body, of His flesh and of His bones. 'For this reason a man shall leave his father and mother and be joined to his wife, and the two shall become one flesh.' This is a great mystery, but I speak concerning Christ and the church..."* **Ephesians 5:29-32**

Our bodies are flesh and bone members of Christ's body. Paul asked the church at Corinth, *"...Shall I then take the members of Christ and make them members of a harlot? Certainly not!..."* *(I Corinthians 6:15)*. In similar manner shall we take the members of Christ and make them infirmed, sick, or diseased? God forbid! We must resist infirmities, sicknesses, and diseases and find the way of the Lord to rid our bodies of them. They have no legal right to us. We belong to Christ! Any infringement in our bodies by them is an illegal trespass. The exception to this understanding is if we create an environment of darkness by what we eat, drink, put into our bodies, or do with our bodies. Then they have legal right to dwell in the darkness we have created.

If we do not have sound doctrine regarding healing, we will most likely accept infirmities, sicknesses, and diseases as just part of being human living here on earth. This device of the enemy is very active on earth to deceive mankind into thinking, *"Everyone gets sick sometime."*. The darker side of the enemy's devices comes more subtly and more craftily in an effort to deceive us into believing infirmities, sicknesses, and diseases are from God. Horrors!

Once we believe healing is the will of God and enter into relationship with Christ as Healer, our resistance against infirmities, sicknesses and diseases can become faith filled, direct, and very aggressive. An inaccurate notion exists that one of the reasons a person may not be able to appropriate healing is because they do not have *"...enough faith..."*. This notion is extremely flawed. Jesus gave His disciples two illustrations of the great power of faith. The first was in relation to casting out a demon. He said to His disciples who asked Him why they were unable to cast a demon out of a little boy, *"Because of your unbelief; for assuredly, I say to you, If you have faith as a mustard seed, you will say to this mountain, 'Move from here to there,' and it will move; and nothing will be impossible for you..."* ***(Matthew 17:20)***.

Appropriating Healing

In the second illustration the apostles said to the Lord, *"...Increase our faith..."*. Then the Lord said, *"...If you have faith as a mustard seed, you can say to this mulberry tree, 'Be pulled up by the roots and be planted in the sea,' and it would obey you..." **(Luke 17:6)***. The understanding we gain from both of these illustrations is not having *"...enough faith..."* is not what prohibits a person from doing the will of God. Jesus said faith even as small as a mustard seed will move mountains and pluck up mulberry trees. The faith our God gave us at the time of our salvation is so powerful it was the agent He used for us to be born again, delivering us from spiritual death.

Faith to appropriate the provisions of the new covenant must be accurately based on sound doctrine according to our knowledge of the will of God. Sound doctrine of Christ as Healer is the means of obtaining *"...faith..."* with which to appropriate healing. *"...So then faith comes by hearing, and hearing by the word of God..."* **Romans 10:17**. Unsound doctrine will abort any effort from anyone endeavoring to appropriate any provision of the new covenant.

After we have established healing is the will of God and entered into relationship with Christ as our Healer, we can speak directly to the infirmity, sickness, or disease trespassing in our body, call it an illegal trespasser, and serve it an eviction notice. Just remember these things steal, kill, and destroy and are not likely to yield without a fight. Whether or not infirmity, sickness, and disease are actual beings, each has a living component that can be seen under a microscope. Their living component is what makes them harmful within our bodies. We can talk directly to the life of the infirmity, sickness, or disease telling it to *"...cease and desist..."* its life force within us.

Even the world understands how disgusting the life of infirmities, sicknesses, and diseases is. Several pharmaceutical companies have television advertisements involving a *"...cold..."* attacking a person. They made the cold awful in appearance which is easy for the public to accept because we all know how grotesque a cold can be in our bodies. Maybe you need to look online for the particular infirmity, sickness, or disease which has trespassed within your body and see photos of the microscopic life of it. Have you ever seen a microscopic photo of pollen? No wonder we sneeze. Our bodies are fighting to get that stuff out of us.

After we have exercised our faith against the infirmity, sickness, or disease, we then begin a rigorous regimen of rejoicing thanking the Lord for depositing healing into the heavenly account. We make it personal. We thank Him for His willingness to shed His blood to provide healing for us. We thank Him for taking this infirmity, sickness, or disease in His own body so we do not have to have it in our body. Our faith and our actions become the *"...healing..."* for which we are hoping, the evidence of it even though we may not be able to see it with our natural eye just yet! This is the will and one of the ways of God to appropriate healing.

Chapter Four

Doubt's Effects on Faith

In Scripture doubt is typically contrasted with faith, and associated with unbelief, but how so? Because we have a faith based covenant with God *(Ephesians 2:8; Galatians 3:15-4:7; Hebrews 10:38; Hebrews 11:1-2)*, we must gain accurate understanding of the contrast doubt has with faith and the type of association it has with unbelief in order to avoid doubt and unbelief. What is doubt? Is it different from unbelief?

Strong's Exhaustive Concordance of the Bible and ***W.E. Vine's Expository Dictionary of New Testament Words*** both consider the English term *"...doubt..."* in one form or another *(i.e. doubt, doubtful, doubting, doubtless)* in the New Testament. There are seven Greek terms common to both ***Strong's*** and ***Vine's*** for which the English term *"...doubt..."* in its various forms was translated. The Greek language is obviously rich in vocabulary to specifically express man's thoughts or feelings. The English language is lacking in its ability to differentiate thoughts or feelings of man regarding various things in our lives. For example, we use a single term *"...love..."* to express how we feel about hamburgers, our families, and God. Of course, use of the term *"...love..."* in these illustrations does not adequately differentiate how we *"...feel..."* about food, our families, or our God.

We must not establish understanding of the things of God with only a definition from a dictionary nor a word study.

Lord of Healing

However, God the Holy Spirit inspired Scripture, and, therefore, we can begin the process of gaining understanding by considering the terms used by the inspired writers of Scripture. Although there are seven Greek terms for which the English term *"...doubt..."* in its various forms was translated, all of them have the concept of *"...doubt..."* as their root. ***Webster's New Universal Unabridged Dictionary*** defines *"...**doubt**..."* as *"...to waver or fluctuate in opinion or belief; to be uncertain or undecided respecting the truth or fact; to be undetermined...".*

What is unbelief? ***Strong's*** lists two Greek terms for which the English term *"...unbelief..."* is translated:

> ***543 apeitheia*** from *545; disbelief* (obstinate and rebellious): -- disobedience, unbelief.

> ***570 apistia*** from *571; faithlessness*, i.e. (neg.) disbelief (*want of* Chr. *faith*), or (pos.) *unfaithfulness* (*disobedience*): -- unbelief.

A person can have *"...unbelief..."* simply because he chooses not to believe or because he is obstinate and rebellious against the truth. Doubt is not unbelief; it is just uncertainty. However, if a person does not believe the word of the Lord, or is obstinate and rebellious against the word, or just doubts, it is because he has a veil on his heart keeping him from seeing the Lord. Any person who turns his heart toward the Lord will have all veils removed, will behold the glory of the Lord, and will be changed by the power of the Spirit of the Lord *(II Corinthians 3:15-18)*. ***He will believe!***

Doubt's Effects on Faith

Immediately following *II Corinthians 3:15-18* Paul wrote...

> *"Therefore, since we have this ministry, as we have received mercy, we do not lose heart. But we have renounced the hidden things of shame, not walking in craftiness nor handling the word of God deceitfully, but by manifestation of the truth commending ourselves to every man's conscience in the sight of God. But even **if our gospel is veiled, it is veiled to those who are perishing, whose minds the god of this age has blinded, who do not believe, lest the light of the gospel of the glory of Christ, who is the image of God should shine on them**. For we do not preach ourselves, but Christ Jesus the Lord, and ourselves your bondservants for Jesus' sake. For it is the God who commanded the light to shine out of darkness, who has shone in our hearts to give the light of the knowledge of the glory of God in the face of Jesus Christ." **II Corinthians 4:1-6***

Our God has made a way for *"...the light of the gospel of the glory of Christ, who is the image of God to shine on them (the lost)..."* as the means for them to believe by the power of His might. No one, absolutely no one has to be restricted to the power of their own might as the means of believing. Everyone can have access to the power of God as the means of believing if they will simply turn their heart toward the Lord who is preached to them.

For any provision of the new covenant, we can remove the veil of doubt or unbelief by turning our heart toward the Lord who is preached to us. Doubt and unbelief will stop the power of God from producing the will of God in our lives. We can and must avoid doubt and unbelief. All it takes is a turn of the heart.

Lord of Healing

Doubt in contrast with faith can be easily illustrated using Peter's faith experience walking on the water *(Matthew 14:23-33)*. *Verses 29 and 30* say, *"...And when Peter had come down out of the boat, he walked on the water to go to Jesus. **But when he saw the wind was boisterous, he was afraid**; and beginning to sink he cried out, saying 'Lord, save me!'..."*.

Doubt typically enters a person's life as a result of some external stimulus. In Peter's experience the external stimulus was the boisterous condition of the wind and waves around him. We must applaud Peter's faith and courage for having been willing to step out of the boat. To applaud his faith and courage does not in any way justify his doubt. Jesus rebuked him for his doubt. However, it is so easy to understand how his experience in a hostile environment created the perfect conditions for doubt. Please do not think harshly of this great man of faith! Instead, we must be thankful the Holy Spirit has given us such a wonderful illustration from whom to learn.

In an effort to appropriate *"...healing..."* external stimuli serving to promote doubt can be lack of relief from symptoms or lack of immediacy in appropriating the healing we desire. Just like the hostile environment of the boisterous wind and waves created perfect conditions for doubt, so, too, the ill effects of infirmity, sickness, and disease create perfect conditions for doubt.

Consider the revelation of enticement and temptation which lead to sin presented by James to help us better understand external stimulus leading to doubt.

Doubt's Effects on Faith

> *"Let no one say when he is tempted, 'I am tempted by God'; for God cannot be tempted by evil, nor does He Himself tempt anyone. But each one is tempted when he is drawn away by his own desires and enticed. Then, when desire has conceived, it gives birth to sin; and sin, when it is full-grown, brings forth death..."*
> **James 1:13-15**

If it is only a person's flesh that desires the thing with which they are being enticed, it is not considered sin from God's perspective. It is what the person does with the desires of his flesh in relation to the enticement that determines if it becomes sin. If the person allows the desires of his flesh to become one with his mind transitioning him out of a spiritually minded state into a carnally minded state, then conception will take place giving birth to sin. Paul wrote to the church at Rome...

> *"...those who live according to the flesh set their minds on the things of the flesh, but those who live according to the spirit, the things of the spirit. For to be carnally minded is death, but to be spiritually minded is life and peace. Because to be carnally minded is death, but to be spiritually minded is life and peace. Because the carnal mind is enmity against God; for it is not subject to the law of God, nor indeed can be."* **Romans 8:5-7**

All born again persons still living on earth have *"...flesh..."* that is not yet glorified. Such unglorified flesh has desires that do not conform to the standards of God. If a person lives according to the flesh, he will set his mind on the things of the flesh making him carnally minded. A carnally minded person lives constantly being drawn away by his own fleshly desires when enticed allowing his fleshly desires to become the desires of his mind. This is the definition of carnally minded.

Jesus was led into the wilderness, fasted for forty days, and was tempted by the devil *(Luke 4:1-13)*. The first temptation the devil sat before Him was to turn a stone into bread *(Luke 4:3)*. Jesus' flesh *"...desired..."* bread because He was at the end of a forty day fast? If His flesh did not *"...desire..."* bread after forty days of fasting, then His flesh was not made like ours. However, Scripture teaches He was made in all ways like us *(except of course for being born of a virgin so as not to partake of Adam's sin)*.

> *"**In as much then as the children have partaken of flesh and blood, He Himself likewise shared in the same**, that through death He might destroy him who had the power of death, that is, the devil, and release those who through fear of death were all their lifetime subject to bondage. For indeed He does not give aid to angels, but He does give aid to the seed of Abraham. Therefore, **in all things He had to be made like His brethren**, that He might be a merciful and faithful High Priest in things pertaining to God, to make propitiation for the sins of the people. For in that **He Himself has suffered, being tempted, He is able to aid those who are tempted.**"*
> **Hebrews 2:14-18**

Jesus' flesh desired bread, but that desire was not sin because He had not chosen to live according to the flesh. Instead, He had chosen to live according to the spirit making Him spiritually minded. As a spiritually minded person He saw the enticement to turn the stone into bread playing on the desire of His flesh as merely a temptation. He was able to resist this temptation because He was not carnally minded. His response to the devil who was tempting Him revealed He had chosen to live after the spirit, setting His mind on the spirit instead of the flesh. He said, *"...It is written, man shall not live by bread alone, but by every word God..." **(Luke 4:4)***. He was tempted but did not sin because as a spiritually minded person He refused to yield to the external stimulus tempting His flesh. The external stimulus did not cause Him to doubt.

There is a progression required in temptation in order for it to lead to sin and death. First is the temptation. It is followed by a person being drawn away by the desires of his own flesh. Next, desire conceives and gives birth to sin. Finally, when sin is full-grown, it brings forth death. Temptation is the doorway through which a person passes leading to sin and death. Doubt is temptation! It is the doorway through which a person passes leading to an abortion of their faith and ultimately into *"...unbelief..."!*

Unbelief is a person's *"...choice..."* not to believe. The writer of the letter to the Hebrew Christians was inspired to write a really remarkable thing regarding *"...unbelief..."*.

> *"Therefore, as the Holy Spirit says:*
>
> > *'Today, if you will hear His voice, do not harden your hearts as in the rebellion, in the day of trial in the wilderness, where your fathers tested Me, tried Me, and saw My works forty years. Therefore I was angry with that generation, and said, 'They always go astray in their heart, and they have not known My ways. So I swore in My wrath, 'They shall not enter My rest.'*

Lord of Healing

> *Beware, brethren, lest there be in any of you **an evil heart of unbelief in departing from the living God**; but exhort one another daily, while it is called 'Today,' lest any of you be hardened through the deceitfulness of sin."*
> ***Hebrews 3:7-13***

Unbelief is not a good thing. Scripture associates unbelief with an evil heart! Doubt is the doorway which leads to *"..unbelief..."*.

Why is unbelief so bad? Why is it associated with an evil heart? If we can gain answers to these questions, they will help us avoid unbelief altogether. During Jesus' earthly ministry He was the perfect expression of the Father. Jesus, born of a virgin without the involvement of a man *(Luke 1:26-56)*, did not have the sin of Adam pass into Him *(Romans 5:12)*. Jesus was a perfect, sinless representative of His Father. He fulfilled His ministry in the anointing of God the Holy Spirit *(Luke 4:16-21)*. He came into the earth to do only the will of His Father, not His own *(John 5:30; John 7:16-19; Matthew 26:39)*. When Jesus spoke the word of God to people, that word was completely free of any and all corruption, empowered with divine ability, and clothed with the very presence of God! Not only did Jesus speak the word of God in such a manner, He demonstrated His oneness with God by the supernatural works He did *(John 14:9-11)*.

Compare an Old Testament illustration to help us gain understanding in these matters. Samuel was a prophet in the Old Testament serving as a type of leader to the Israelites providing them the word of the Lord as guidance for their lives and their nation. However, the people desired a change of

Doubt's Effects on Faith

leadership. They went to the prophet Samuel and said, *"Look, you are old, and your sons do not walk in your ways. Now make us a king to judge us like all the nations." (I Samuel 8:5)*. The next verse revealed *"...the thing displeased Samuel...So Samuel prayed to the Lord..." (I Samuel 8:6)*. The Lord's response to Samuel is very revealing.

> *"...And the Lord said to Samuel, 'Heed the voice of the people in all that they say to you;* ***for they have not rejected you, but they have rejected Me, that I should not reign over them****. According to all the works which they have done since the day that I brought them up out of Egypt, even to this day -- with which they have forsaken Me and served other gods --* ***so they are doing to you also****..." I Samuel 8:7,8*

Scripture is clear in *verses seven and eight* the people were actually rejecting God, not the man called by God sent to speak the word of God to the people of God. This is extremely significant in developing an understanding of how unbelief is associated with an evil heart.

Even though Jesus was free of any and all corruption, a pure, sinless, anointed, representative of God, clothed in the very presence of God, the people to whom He was sent rejected Him just like they rejected Samuel. God said the Israelite's rejection of Samuel, the one He had sent, was actually rejecting Him. So, too, then the people's rejection of Jesus, the One God sent, was actually rejecting the One who sent Him? When the people rejected Christ, they were rejecting God His Father! How is it possible for anyone to reject Christ as the only means to eternal and everlasting life? ...the only means to the Father *(John 14:6)*? Because they do not believe!

Lord of Healing

Paul addressed this very issue in his second letter to the church at Corinth.

> "*...if our gospel is veiled, it is veiled to those who are perishing, whose minds the god of this age has blinded,* who do not believe, lest the light of the gospel of the glory of Christ, who is the image of God, should shine on them. For we do not preach ourselves, but Christ Jesus the Lord, and ourselves your bondservants for Jesus' sake. For it is the God who commanded light to shine out of darkness, who has shone in our hearts to give the light of the knowledge of the glory of God in the face of Jesus Christ." **II Corinthians 4:4-6**

A person will reject Christ because his mind has been blinded by the god of this age. How does the god of this age blind a person's mind to keep him from seeing and believing in Christ? Is the enemy that powerful? More powerful than the gospel? More powerful than the anointing? More powerful than the word of God? Powerful enough to arbitrarily *"...blind the mind..."* of a person to keep him from seeing and believing?

In this same second letter to the church at Corinth, *II Corinthians 3*, Paul was inspired to write that if a person is blind to the truth, it is because he has a veil on his heart *(II Corinthians 3:7-18)*. *Verse 16* says, *"...Nevertheless when one turns to the Lord, the veil is taken away..."*. Whether or not a person has a veil on his heart is determined by whether the person has his heart turned toward the Lord. If a person will turn his heart toward the Lord, all veils will be removed and the person will behold the glory of the Lord and be changed by the Spirit of the Lord.

Doubt's Effects on Faith

The god of this age can only blind the mind of a person if that person refuses to turn his heart toward the Lord. These conditions of the heart, *"...not turned toward the Lord..."*, and *"...blindness of mind..."* do not only apply to the lost who are *"...strangers from the covenants of promise, having no hope and without God in the world..." (**Ephesians 2:12**)*. They can also apply to those who have been born again.

Consider the church at Laodicea whom Jesus rebuked. Jesus loved this church very much.

> *"And to the angel of the church of the Laodiceans write, 'These things says the Amen, the Faithful and True Witness, the Beginning of the creation of God: I know your works, that you are neither cold nor hot. I could wish you were cold or hot. So then, because you are lukewarm, and neither cold nor hot, I will vomit you out of My mouth. Because **you say, 'I am rich, have become wealthy, and have need of nothing' -- and do not know that you are wretched, miserable, poor, blind, and naked** -- I counsel you to buy from Me gold refined in the fire, that you may be rich; and white garments, that you may be clothed, that the shame of your nakedness may not be revealed; and anoint your eyes with eye salve, that you may see. As many as I love, I rebuke and chasten. Therefore be zealous and repent..."*
> ***Revelation 3:14-19***

This is one of the most extreme cases in Scripture of believers who had become so carnally minded Jesus actually called them *"...blind..."*. Instead of remaining spiritually minded after their new birth, they shifted their desires back to the things their flesh desired, making them carnally minded *(See **Romans 8:5-7**)*. A person who lives according to the flesh has a veil over his heart and is easy prey for the devices of the enemy to blind him. The only way to have the veil removed is for the person to turn his heart toward the Lord and repent so he can see again. Jesus said of the Laodiceans, *"...you say, 'I am rich, have become wealthy, and have need of nothing'..."*. It is easy to see how such a condition in born again people can be described as *"...blind..."!* They could not even *"...see..."* their need for Jesus. They said they had *"...need of nothing...".*

Scripture declares, *"...out of the abundance of the heart the mouth speaks..." (**Matthew 12:34**)*. What the Laodiceans *"...spoke..."* was out of the abundance of their heart, hearts clearly not turned toward the Lord. A condition Jesus referred to as *"...blind..."*, and one we can easily see as *"...unbelief..."!*

God is not requiring us to *"...believe..."* anything and everything a person preaches or teaches. Our faith is to be based solidly on the living Word, the written word, witness of the word born by the Holy Spirit, and confirmation of the word from brethren who are approved to God *(**II Timothy 2:15**)*. If we will turn our hearts toward the Lord desiring to know Him through the word preached, we will know the truth of whatever revelation is given to us. Any veil of doubt and the doorway to unbelief it represents will be removed. We will behold the Lord and believe! Doubt's effects on our faith will be removed so we will be able to *"...walk by faith and not by sight..."!*

Chapter Five
Laying on of Hands

"...Laying on of hands..." is included in the list of *"...basic principles of the doctrine of Christ..." (**Hebrews 6:1**)* as one of the foundation stones upon which our lives are to be built. It is not only supernaturally powerful, but it is also an extremely personal part of the design of God for our lives. God has chosen for us to lay our hands on the infirmed as one of the ways they may receive healing. Why did He include a means of healing involving *"...touch..."*? While there are surely various answers, Scripture provides us with an illustration of healing involving touch which helps our understanding.

In the account of the woman with the issue of blood in the New Testament, Jesus spoke only a few words, but they were full of revelation about touch in the process of healing.

> *"Now a woman, having a flow of blood for twelve years, who had spent all her livelihood on physicians and could not be healed by any, came from behind and **touched the border of His garment. And immediately her flow of blood stopped**. And Jesus said, 'Who touched Me?' When all denied it, Peter and those with him said, 'Master, the multitudes throng and press You, and You say, 'Who touched Me?' But Jesus said, **'Somebody touched Me, for I perceived power going out from Me.'** Now when the woman saw that she was not hidden, she came trembling; and falling down before Him, she declared to Him in the presence of all the people the reason she had touched Him and how she was healed immediately.*

Lord of Healing

And He said to her, 'Daughter, be of good cheer; your faith has made you well. Go in peace." **Luke 4:43-48**

After this woman *"...**touched** the border of His garment. And immediately her flow of blood stopped..."* Jesus said, *"... 'Somebody **touched** Me, for I perceived **power (1411)** going out from Me.'..."*.

> *1411 dunamis* from *1410; force* (lit. or fig.); spec. miraculous power (usually by impl. a *miracle* itself): -- ability, abundance, meaning, might (-ily, -y, -y deed), (worker of) miracle (-a), power, strength, violence, mighty (wonderful) work.

The **New King James** version of the Bible translates this Greek term *"...dunamis..."* using the English word *"...power..."*. The **King James** version of the Bible translates this same Greek term *"...dunamis..."* using the English word *"...virtue..."*. No matter which one of these English words is used, when the woman *"...touched the border of Jesus' garment..."* **something** actually flowed out from Him. What was it? Whatever it was, it healed her of an incurable issue of blood with which she had suffered for twelve years.

During His earthly ministry Jesus said very plainly, *"...the Son (Jesus) can do nothing of Himself..." **(John 5:19,30)**.* In the synagogue on a certain Sabbath Jesus read from the scroll of the prophet Isaiah. In the New Testament this account of Jesus reading from Isaiah can be found in ***Luke 4:18-20**.*

> *"So He (Jesus) came to Nazareth, where He had been brought up. And as His custom was, He went into the synagogue on the Sabbath day, and stood up to read. And He was handed the book of the prophet Isaiah. And*

Laying on of Hands

when He had opened the book, He found the place where it was written:

> *'The Spirit of the Lord is upon Me, because he has anointed Me to heal the brokenhearted, to proclaim liberty to the captives and recovery of sight to the blind, to set at liberty those who are oppressed; to proclaim the acceptable year of the Lord.'*

*Then He closed the book, and gave it back to the attendant and sat down. And the eyes of all who were in the synagogue were fixed on Him. And He began to say to them, **'Today this Scripture is fulfilled in your hearing'**..." Luke 4:18-21*

When Jesus said, "... *'Today this Scripture is fulfilled in your hearing...'*", He was telling the people He was the person about whom Isaiah was prophesying. Jesus is the Anointed One!

Jesus had chosen to divest Himself of His divine attributes and live on the earth as a man in order to redeem us *(Hebrews 2:14,17)*. Jesus who said, *"...the Son (Jesus) can do nothing of Himself..." (John 5:19,30)*, also said the Holy Spirit was the means by which He fulfilled His ministry. Whether He was preaching, teaching, healing, or delivering people, everything He did was by the Holy Spirit. In the account of the woman with the issue of blood when Jesus said *"... 'Somebody touched Me, for I perceived power going out from Me.'..."*, the power going out from Him was the power of the Holy Spirit.

Scripture teaches, *"...When she heard about Jesus, she came behind Him in the crowd and touched His garment. For she said, **'If only I may touch His clothes, I shall be made well.'"** (Mark 5:27,28)*. She believed making contact with Jesus, merely the garments on His body, would make her well. After the healing process was complete, Jesus said, *"...your faith has made you well..." (**Mark 4:34**)*. Believing *"...If only I may touch His clothes, I shall be made well...."* and actually touching His clothes was the way she expressed her faith. But, how did this expression of faith work?

She believed Jesus was the source of healing. However, Jesus said *"...the Son (Jesus) can do nothing of Himself..." (**John 5:19,30**)*. Jesus spoke plainly how the Holy Spirit had anointed Him as the means of fulfilling His earthly ministry. When the woman touched the border of Jesus' garment, her faith activated the anointing which flowed out from His body, entered her body, and healed her. In a book I wrote previously, entitled **Holy Spirit Unveiled**, there is an entire chapter devoted to the anointing. In that chapter the anointing was revealed as *"...who..."*, not *"...what..."*. The Holy Spirit is the anointing *(See **I John 2:27; John 14:15-17,26; John 15:26; John 16:7-13**)*.

While not required, the woman with the issue of blood needed a point of contact in order for her to exercise her faith to appropriate healing. Touching the border of Jesus' garment was not a ceremonial act. It provided a point of release for the woman according to her faith allowing healing to flow into her. There is no Scriptural evidence she knew it would be the Holy Spirit who would be the healing power that would heal her. Her faith in Jesus was enough to activate the healing power resident within Him to heal her.

Laying on of Hands

Touch is not required in order for a person to appropriate healing. Although God has given us *"...laying on of hands..."* as one means of receiving healing, it is not required, only available. The woman was not required to touch the border of Jesus' garment. That was merely what she needed as a point of contact to exercise her faith. Thank God for His love and gracious benevolence to connect with any person willing to exercise faith toward Him.

This woman's *"...faith touch..."* activated the healing power within Jesus and started it flowing into her. Couldn't *"...virtue..."* have flowed into the woman without her touching Jesus' garment? Yes, as we have already stated touch is not required to receive healing, but in this dispensation the Holy Spirit has chosen to operate within the parameters of our faith according to our knowledge of the will of God. Of course, that does not exclude the possibility of the Holy Spirit operating in the Sovereign disposition as God at any time.

The Holy Spirit is one of the three parts of the Triune Sovereign God. As Sovereign, God can do anything He wills. However, in this dispensation the Triune God has revealed the priority of His will is to work in conjunction with the faith of people according to their knowledge of His will *(See **Chapter Two**, **pages 13-16**)*. This woman *"...heard about **Jesus**, she came behind Him in the crowd, and touched His garment. For she said, '**If only I may touch His clothes, I shall be made well.**" (Mark 5:27,28)*. Her knowledge was of Jesus, not the Holy Spirit. The Holy Spirit awaited the expression of her faith, *"...touching..."* Jesus, before His power flowed into her to heal her.

Lord of Healing

Consider what Paul wrote in his letter to the church at Rome about the diversity of gifts given by God to the church in relation to the will of God operating according to our faith, *"...Having then gifts differing according to the grace that is given to us, let us use them: if prophecy,* ***let us prophesy in proportion to our faith****... (**Romans 12:6**)*. Here instructions are given for a person to prophesy, a provision of the church a person would know to be the will of God, in proportion to his faith.

It is written in the Old Testament, God *"...opened the mouth of the donkey, and she said to Balaam..." (**Numbers 22:28**)*. It is always the prerogative of God to exercise His sovereign power, even to make a donkey speak. He could exercise His sovereign power to cause any of us to speak His word at any time, just like the donkey. We are, nevertheless, instructed to prophesy according to the proportion of faith we know we have. He has chosen to work in conjunction with the faith of people, especially so in the new covenant, although His sovereign will is always His option.

It was the will of God for Jesus to divest Himself of His divine attributes and to live as a man during His earthly ministry. It was the will of God for the Holy Spirit to anoint Jesus as the means for Him to be able to fulfill His ministry while living on earth. It was and is the will of God for the Holy Spirit to provide His ministry to us in conjunction with our faith according to our knowledge of the will of God.

The woman with the issue of blood *"...touched the border of Jesus' garment..."* according to her faith so she could appro-

Laying on of Hands

priate healing. Touch in the woman's case was initiated by the infirmed person desiring to be healed. How does *"...laying on of hands..."* which involves touch initiated by the non-infirmed person operate? *"...**Principally the same**..."* The woman's *"...touch..."* provided a point of contact through which the *"...power..."* could flow out of Jesus and into her for her to be healed. When a believer lays hands on an infirmed person, the one laying on hands is creating a point of contact through which the power from the Holy Spirit can flow out of them and into the infirmed.

Consider a natural world illustration. Electricity is available within the wiring of our homes all the time. A person can activate the electricity in any room of their house by simply flipping a switch which will in turn provide light in that room. If a person needs benefit from an appliance requiring electricity as its power source, the person can push the end of the electrical cord attached to the appliance into an outlet and the electricity will be immediately available to power the appliance. Our daily lives in the natural world are filled with these types of illustrations. The person flipping the switch or plugging in the appliance is not the electricity; they are merely the agent by whom the electricity is activated.

When a believer lays hands on, he is not the healing power; he is merely the agent exercising his faith to activate the healing power. We must be very careful using this illustration so we do not fall into the trap of tradition and the doctrine of man. We must not see any of the members of the Trinity as something we are to *"...use..."* for our gain. We certainly must not see the Holy Spirit as the *"...power..."* of God we simply flip a switch to activate.

> ***The Holy Spirit is not the power of God.***
> ***He is "...a person..." who is God***
> ***and He "...has power..."!***

The difference is monumental. One understanding will lead us to try to find a switch to flip that we may *"...use..."* the Holy Spirit. The other will lead us to develop relationship with Him that we may learn how to work together with Him. *"...The people who know their God will be strong and do great exploits."* ***Daniel 11:32****!*

When a believer *"...lays hands on..."* the sick, the believer must understand *"...laying on of hands..."* is not a ceremonial act. The believer must understand the laying on of hands provides a point of contact through which the power from the Holy Spirit can flow out of us and into the infirmed person to heal them. This is an act of faith to be done in cooperation with God the Holy Spirit!

Chapter Six
Faith to Receive

In *Chapter Four* we presented an understanding of *"...doubt..."* and *"...unbelief...".* Now we need to consider *"...faith...".* Doubt, unbelief, and faith all three exist in relation to a person's knowledge of the word of God. Doubt is uncertainty about the word. Unbelief is a conscious choice not to believe or even an obstinate rebellion against the word. What then is *"...faith..."* in relation to the word?

In Paul's letter to the church at Ephesus, he wrote our very salvation comes *"...through faith..."* . Faith is an essential part of our lives in the new covenant!

> *"For by grace you have been saved through **faith**, and that not of yourselves; it is the gift of God, not of works, lest anyone should boast."* **Ephesians 2:8**

Paul was inspired to reveal a powerful understanding about *"...faith..."* in relation to our salvation and the word in his letter to the church at Rome.

> *"For whoever calls on the name of the Lord shall be saved. How then shall they call on Him in whom they have not believed? And how shall they believe in Him of whom they have not heard? And how shall they hear without a preacher? And how shall they preach unless they are sent? As it is written:*

Lord of Healing

> *'How beautiful are the feet of those who preach the gospel of peace, who bring glad tidings of good things!'*
>
> *But they have not all obeyed the gospel. For Isaiah says, 'Lord, who has believed our report?"* ***So then faith comes by hearing, and hearing by the word of God."***
> ***Romans 10:13-17***

Faith is a gift from God given as the means by which we are to be saved *(II Corinthians 5:7; Galatians 3:15-4:7)*. This faith gift from God comes to all who have their heart turned toward the Lord as they hear the word regarding Jesus as the source of salvation. The old covenant was based on man's ability to see, understand, and do the will of God. The new covenant is based on faith as the ability God gives us to see, understand, and do His will.

All men have natural faith, but the faith by which men are saved is not natural faith. Saving faith comes by hearing the word of God *(Romans 10:17)*. Natural man cannot receive the things of the spirit of God *(I Corinthians 2:9-16)*. All men do not have saving faith *(II Thessalonians 3:1,2)* because they have either not heard the word of salvation, or they have heard but refused to turn their heart toward the Lord so He could provide them the ability to *"...hear..."* and receive faith.

With natural faith we are able to sit down in a chair believing it will not collapse with us in it. Natural faith is a type of faith, but it cannot be used to appropriate salvation nor any of the provisions of the new covenant. Only with the faith-gift from God can we be born again and appropriate the provisions of the kingdom.

Faith to Receive

The faith we have from God is divinely empowered, and with it we will be able to do all God wills in our lives! God could have chosen an infinite number of ways for us to be able to appropriate the provisions of the new covenant, but He chose *"...faith..."*. Jesus said if our faith is only the size of a mustard seed, we will be able to move mountains and pluck up trees. Appropriating new covenant provisions, moving mountains, or plucking up trees are all possible because the faith God gives is *divinely empowered!*

The priority for our lives is to accept the revelation that we *"...have been saved by grace through faith; it is a gift from God..." (**Ephesians 2:8**)*, that *"...faith comes by hearing, and hearing by the word of God..." (**Romans 10:17**)*, and that *"...if you have faith as a mustard seed, you will say to this mountain, 'Move from here to there,' and it will move; and nothing will be impossible for you..." (**Matthew 17:20**)*. Divinely empowered faith causing us to be born again, move mountains, or pluck up trees *(**Luke 17:6**)* will most certainly enable us to receive healing. But how does *"...faith..."* come by which to be healed?

Consider the Scriptural reference regarding *"...whoever calls on the name of the Lord shall be saved..." (**Romans 10:13**)*. Very specific questions require very specific answers in order for a person to be able to call on the name of the Lord to be saved.

> *"How then shall they call on Him in whom they have not believed? And how shall they believe in Him of whom they have not heard? And how shall they hear without a preacher? And how shall they preach unless they are sent?"* **Romans 10:14,15**

Lord of Healing

Faith is very specific in nature. Faith to be saved comes by hearing the word regarding *"...who..."* Jesus is as the source of salvation *(Romans 10:9-17)*. In order to obtain faith to appropriate any of the provisions of the new covenant, we must hear specifically who Jesus is as the source of the provision we seek.

In order for faith to come so we may be able to receive *"...healing..."* we can apply the same Scriptural standard required to receive salvation. We called on Jesus as Lord to be saved. In order to be *"...healed..."*, we must call on Christ as Healer.

> *"How then shall they call on Him in whom they have not believed? And how shall they believe in Him of whom they have not heard? And how shall they hear without a preacher? And how shall they preach unless they are sent?...So then, faith comes by hearing, and hearing by the word of God"* **Romans 10:14,15,17**

We will only be able to believe in Christ as Healer if we have heard of Him as Healer. We will have heard of Him as Healer because someone preached Him as Healer. Someone preached Christ as Healer because they were sent to do so. Of course, this Scriptural standard *(Romans 10:13-17)* does not exclude the possibility of a person studying on their own and hearing directly from the Holy Spirit that Jesus is the source of healing. However, whether someone preached to us or we studied and heard on our own; *"...faith comes by hearing, and hearing by the word of God..." (Romans 10:17)*.

Faith to Receive

Faith is being agreed with God! We are only able to agree with God and the particular revelation from His word we are receiving because He gives us the ability to do so. *"Faith is a gift from God, not of works, lest anyone should boast."* **Ephesians 2:8,9.**

Consider the Scriptural account of Jesus sending out His twelve disciples with very specific authority and instructions to illustrate this understanding.

> *"And when He (Jesus) had called His twelve disciples to Him, He gave them power over unclean spirits, to cast them out, and to heal all kinds of sicknesses and diseases. ...These twelve Jesus sent out and commanded them, saying, 'Do not go into the way of the Gentiles, and do not enter a city of the Samaritans. but go rather to the lost sheep of the house of Israel. And as you go, preach, saying, 'The kingdom of heaven is at hand.' Heal the sick, cleanse the lepers, raise the dead, cast out demons. Freely you have received, freely give.'..."*
> **Matthew 10:1,5-8** *(entire context **verses 1-42**)*

In *Mark 6:7-13* we see a parallel record of Jesus calling the twelve to Himself sending them out and giving *"...them power over unclean spirits..."*. Mark's account adds, *"And they (the twelve) cast out many demons..." (**Mark 6:13**)*.

In *Matthew 17:14-21* a man brought his son to Jesus saying, *"Lord, have mercy on my son, for he is an epileptic and suffers severely; for he often falls into the fire and often into the water. So I brought him to Your disciples, but they could not cure him." (**Matthew 17:15,16**)*. Although the twelve disciples did *"...cast out many demons..." (**Mark 6;13**)*, they could not cast the demon out of this man's son. Jesus' response to this situation is *captivating!*

Lord of Healing

> *"Then Jesus answered and said, 'O faithless and perverse generation, how long shall I be with you? How long shall I bear with you? Bring him here to Me.' And Jesus rebuked the demon, and it came out of him; and the child was cured from that very hour. Then the disciples came to Jesus privately and said, 'Why could we not cast it out?' So Jesus said to them, 'Because of your unbelief; for assuredly, I say to you, if you have faith as a mustard seed, you will say to this mountain, 'Move from here to there,' and it will move; and nothing will be impossible for you."* **Matthew 17:17-20**

When the disciples asked Jesus why they could not cast out the demon, Jesus said, *"...Because of your unbelief..."*. When Jesus sent out the disciples and *"...gave them power over unclean spirits, to cast them out..."*, they were in agreement with Him to go and to do as He said. Jesus' disciples were in agreement with Him that He had authority from God to give them power over unclean spirits and responsibility to cast out demons.

Every one of the many demons they cast out was a direct result of the disciples' agreement with Jesus to do so. Then a demon refused to yield to their power and would not come out. The demon's refusal to yield to their power served as an external stimulus tempting them to doubt, and they yielded. Their doubt became a doorway leading them to unbelief, aborting their faith. Essentially, they stopped agreeing with Jesus that He had authority from God to give them power over demons or to send them to cast out demons: Therefore, leaving them to conclude that they did not have power to cast out demons. Their lack of agreement, which is unbelief, aborted their faith causing them to not be able to cast out demons. Unbelief is a person's choice not to believe. So, just like the

Faith to Receive

church at Laodicea, the twelve disciples chose not to believe *(Matthew 17:20)*, to no longer be in agreement with Jesus.

Whenever a person hears a revelation of Christ regarding some provision of the new covenant, he will do one of three things:

1. He will be uncertain of it because his heart is not turned toward the Lord. *(doubt)*.

2. He will choose not to believe it or to be obstinately rebellious against it because his heart is not turned toward the Lord *(unbelief)*.

3. He will receive faith as a result of hearing because his heart is turned toward the Lord *(faith)*.

The hearer who receives faith comes into agreement with God and His word! Although written as a rhetorical question the eternal wisdom of God asks, *"Can two walk together, except they be agreed?"* ***Amos 3:3***. It is impossible to walk together with God unless we are in agreement with Him! Even after a person has received faith and walked with God according to that faith, he can at any time choose to doubt it, not to believe it, or to become obstinate and rebellious against it. The church at Laodicea *(Revelation 3:14-19)* served to illustrate such a choice as we have already seen in ***Chapter Three, page 47***, as also do the twelve disciples' *"...unbelief..."* in ***Matthew 17:17-20*** regarding casting out demons.

Lord of Healing

Applying these things to receive any revelation from God simplifies our understanding. When someone preaches the word, we are given an opportunity to receive or reject it. For example, suppose someone preaches revelation regarding the *"...eternal redemption..." (A revelation considered in **Chapter One**, pages 4, 6, & 10)*.

> "Jesus' blood is the means by which *"...eternal redemption..."* was wrought **(Hebrews 9:12)**. Every drop of the *"...Lamb's..."* blood shed at the time of His death, whether produced by the stripes on His back from the cruel Roman whip, the violent beatings He was made to endure, the crown of thorns placed on His head, the nails driven in His hands and feet, or the spear thrust into His side, every drop of it was the *"...blood..."* necessary to secure our *"...eternal redemption...";"* **Chapter One, page 10**

If we turn our heart toward the Lord as we receive this word, *"...faith..."* will come as a result of hearing, and we will enter agreement with God regarding the *"...eternal redemption..."!* We will be agreed that every drop of the Lamb's blood shed at the time of His death was the *"...blood..."* necessary to redeem us from the power of darkness *(**Colossians 1:13; Ephesians 6:12**)* and that includes infirmities, sicknesses, and diseases *(**Matthew 8:16,17; Galatians 3:13; I Peter 2:24**)*. We know these things steal, kill, and destroy which Jesus said are *"...works of the thief..." (**John 10:10**)*. Once we have faith and agreement with God and His word regarding Christ as the source of healing, then, and only then, are we ready to receive healing by faith.

Chapter Seven
Patience to Receive

In *Chapter Four* we considered how doubt typically enters a person's life as a result of some external stimulus. In faith's effort to appropriate healing, lack of relief from symptoms or lack of immediacy of healing in our bodies illustrate just such types of stimuli. It is easy for any person who has experienced either of these to understand how both of them could promote doubt. Increasing our understanding of faith to receive healing will help us deal with these stimuli more effectively keeping them from adversely affecting our faith.

The Free Medical Dictionary by *Farlex Online* defines *"...healing..."* as *"...the process of returning to health; the restoration of structure and function of injured or diseased tissues...".* We have all most likely suffered from injured or diseased tissue which needed to be restored to normal structure or function. We understand that *"...process..."* is involved in healing. *Healing is normally not instantaneous!*

Several Greek terms for which the English word *"...healing..."* can be used for translation all contain similar components of meaning: *cure, heal, make whole.* Although Scriptural records of healings mostly show them as immediate, we must not exclude ***process*** from healing. When a believer exercises faith to appropriate healing as part of the eternal redemption paid for by the blood of the Lamb, we do not always see immediate restoration of structure and function of the injured or diseased tissues in the person's body. ***We must allow process to be included in healing!*** The duration of the process is based on variables beyond the believer's control. The only thing which is in the believer's control is his willingness to remain in faith agreeing with God and His word while receiving healing.

Scripture says, *"Now faith is the substance of things hoped for, the evidence of things not seen." **(Hebrews 11:1)**.* Paul wrote in his letter to the church at Rome *"...hope that is seen is not hope; for why does one still hope for what he sees? But if we hope for what we do not see, we eagerly wait for it with perseverance..." **(Romans 8:24,25)***. ***Faith and hope are inextricably linked!***

Successful exercise of faith requires hope. If we exercise our faith to appropriate healing, then hope for healing to become ours is required. New covenant *"...hope..."* is not a wish. Wishes are fantasy based, like making a wish when you blow out candles on a birthday cake. Hope is based on revelation of the will of God. We can only exercise faith to obtain a provision of the new covenant we know to be the will of God. We may not immediately see the provision for which we are exercising our faith, but that is the nature of faith and hope! The time component involved in this process is beyond our control! We are to simply remain patiently in faith until we can see the provision for which we are hoping. Once we can see it, we will no longer need to exercise our faith or hope for it *"...hope that is seen is not hope; for why does one still hope for what he sees? But if we hope for what we do not see, we eagerly wait for it with perseverance..." **(Romans 8:24,25)**.*

Patience to Receive

The time variable involved in this faith-to-receive healing process creates an environment just like the boisterous wind and waves in Peter's water-walking-experience. Jesus could have immediately calmed the wind and waves around Peter, but He did not. Jesus could remove the time component in our faith-to-receive healing process so we receive the healing immediately, but most times He does not. ***Our priority is to exercise faith according to our knowledge of the will of God. Certainty of the will of God will bolster our faith against any stimulus trying to promote doubt.***

Every provision of the new covenant is an expression of the love of God as Jesus told Nicodemus, *"...for God so loved the world that He gave..." (**John 3:16**)*! God loves us and has made provision for us to be able to experience His love. Abba provided the Lamb who gave His *"...blood..."* as the means to obtain *"...eternal redemption..." (**Hebrews 9:12**)* for us all! While there are surely any number of reasons why the time component exists in any of our faith-to-receive experiences, we can be absolutely certain God is not withholding the provision nor tempting us in any way because *"...God cannot be tempted by evil, nor does He Himself tempt anyone..." (**James 1:13**)*.

We must be very careful not to allow anything other than God and His word to define who He is or what type of relationship we are to have with Him. Traditions and the doctrines of men too often attempt to do both but are not always based on the word and will of God. Certain scribes and Pharisees from Jerusalem challenged Jesus with tradition.

Lord of Healing

> *"Why do Your disciples transgress the tradition of the elders? For they do not wash their hands when they eat bread."* **Matthew 15:2** *(entire context **Matthew 15:1-9**)*

Jesus' response was stinging and direct.

> *"...you have made the commandment of God of no effect by your tradition. 'Hypocrites! Well did Isaiah prophesy about you, saying:*
>
>> *'These people draw near to Me with their mouth, and honor Me with their lips, but their heart is far from Me. And in vain they worship Me, teaching as doctrines the commandments of men.'..."* **Matthew 15:6-9**

No tradition or doctrine of man has a right to ascend to the same level of authority as God. God and God alone is Sovereign, and Christ is to have the *"...preeminence..."* over all *(**Ephesians 1:15-23; Philippians 2:5-11; Colossians 1:15-18**)!* The word of God is abundantly clear in these matters!

> *'God resists the proud, but gives grace to the humble.'*
>
> *"Therefore humble yourselves under the mighty hand of God, that He may exalt you in due time, casting all your care upon Him, for He cares for you. Be sober, be vigilant; because your adversary the devil walks about like a roaring lion, seeking whom he may devour. Resist him, steadfast in the faith..."* **I Peter 5:5-9**

With our heart turned toward the Lord when we receive a revelation of God, His word, and His will, we obtain the foundation for our faith. *"Faith comes by hearing, and hearing by the word of God."* **Romans 10:17**. The revelation we receive

Patience to Receive

must have Scriptural support, Holy Spirit affirmation, and confirmation from the brethren who are approved unto God able to rightly divide the word of truth. As we have already stated, *"Our priority is to exercise faith according to our knowledge of the will of God. Certainty of the will of God will bolster our faith against any stimulus trying to promote doubt."*

An ***humble submission*** to God and to the revelation of His word is our first step toward appropriating healing or any other provision of the new covenant. Once our faith is anchored in God regarding a provision, we are to *"...Be sober, be vigilant; because your adversary the devil walks about like a roaring lion, seeking whom he may devour. Resist **(436)** him, steadfast in the faith..." **(I Peter 5:8,9)**.*

> *We are to "...resist..." the devil!*

436 anthistemi from *473* and *2476*; to *stand against,* i.e. *oppose*: -- resist, withstand.

Strong's Exhaustive Concordance of the Bible

resist

1. to stand against,; to withstand; to oppose; to fend off; to withstand the action of.
2. to oppose actively; to strive, fight, argue or work against; to endeavor to counteract or defeat.
3. to keep from yielding to, being affected by, or enjoying; as, she tried to resist temptation.

Webster's New Universal Unabridged Dictionary

Lord of Healing

Resisting the devil is vital. The manner of our resistance needs to conform to Scriptural precedent. Scripture provides us with a record of Jesus Himself being tempted by the devil in the wilderness *(Luke 4:1-13)*. What a wonderful example for us to follow!

The devil tempted Jesus with three temptations. All three temptations challenged Jesus' knowledge of the word. Jesus *"..resisted...." (actively argued against)* the devil in each of the three temptations by *"...speaking..."* directly to him what He *(Jesus)* knew the word of God to be. When the devil offered *"...all the authority and glory of the kingdoms of the world..."* to Jesus in exchange for Jesus' worship, Jesus said *"...Get behind Me, Satan!..." (Luke 4:8)*, and then quoted what had been written as the word of God. This was the only verbal exchange between Jesus and Satan in which Jesus said anything other than quote the word of God.

We are going to be tempted to abandon our faith *"...because your adversary the devil walks about like a roaring lion, seeking whom he may devour!..."*. When we are tempted, not *if* we are, but **when** we are, we must *"...resist..." (actively argue against)* anything which does not conform to our knowledge of God, His word, and His will. In order to do so we must remain within the Scriptural precedent set by Jesus Himself.

Be careful not to go on a wild tirade *(tirade is defined by **Webster** as - a prolonged outburst of bitter, outspoken denunciation)* against the devil. Jesus Himself did not even do that! Remain *"...**humble and submitted**..."* to God and just follow

Jesus' pattern. Say what you know to be the will and word of God. If you are going to follow Jesus' pattern you must *"...say..."* what you know the will and word of God to be, not just think it.

Because our words come out of the abundance of our heart *(Matthew 12:34)*, make certain you are speaking spiritually minded, not carnally minded. Keep it simple like Jesus did in His temptation. Your words, coming out of the abundance of your heart, will not only serve as anointed, accurate, and *"...resistance of..."* (active argument against) the devil, they will also serve to encourage and strengthen your faith.

In Paul's second letter to the church at Corinth he was inspired to write about our resistance. In this letter he elevated the terminology of our resistance to a level called warfare.

> *"For though we walk in the flesh, we do not war according to the flesh. For the weapons of our warfare are not carnal but mighty in God for pulling down strongholds, casting down arguments and every high thing that exalts itself against the knowledge of God, bringing every thought into captivity to the obedience of Christ..."*
> **II Corinthians 10:3-5**

Our weapons, which are mighty in God, are *"...for pulling down strongholds, casting down arguments and every high thing that exalts itself against the knowledge of God, and bring every thought into captivity to the obedience of Christ..."*. We cannot rule out the possibility that these strongholds and arguments may originate through some external source. However, just as liquid poured into a funnel all flows down into a small opening, so, too, strongholds and arguments, no matter where they originate, ultimately flow down into our own thoughts. Our priority is to have our thoughts anchored in God, His word, and His will, which will always be the standard for our lives.

Following Jesus' example of resistance against Satan, the mainstay of His resistance was His knowledge of God, His word, and His will. The priority of our resistance must be the same! Any stronghold, argument, or thought which contradicts our knowledge of God must be pulled or cast down.

In the Garden of Eden Satan spoke directly to Eve planting thoughts in her in an effort to make his thoughts rise above her knowledge of God. However, the sources of strongholds, arguments, or thoughts leading to doubt do not have to be demonic. Lack of relief from symptoms caused by an infirmity or lack of immediacy of receiving healing both create environments which promote doubt. Doubts try to exalt themselves above our knowledge of God. If they are successful, we will choose not to believe and abort our faith.

The weapons of our warfare are not natural. They are supernatural, and mighty in God! Speaking God's word in faith out of a humble heart will release the anointing to break the yoke *(Isaiah 10:27)* and the enemy will flee *(James 4:7)*, just like in Jesus' temptation *(Luke 4:13)*.

Paul was again inspired to write about our resistance in even more specific terms of warfare, armor, and categories of enemies in his letter to the church at Ephesus.

Patience to Receive

"Finally, my brethren, be strong in the Lord and in the power of His might. Put on the whole armor of God, that you may be able to stand against the wiles of the devil. For we do not wrestle against flesh and blood, but against principalities, against powers, against the rulers of the darkness of this age, against spiritual hosts of wickedness in the heavenly places. Therefore take up the whole armor of God, that you may be able to withstand in the evil day, and having done all, to stand. Stand therefore, having girded your waist with truth, having put on the breastplate of righteousness, and having shod your feet with the preparation of the gospel of peace; above all, taking the shield of faith with which you will be able to quench all the fiery darts of the wicked one. And take the helmet of salvation, and the sword of the Spirit, which is the word of God; praying always with all prayer and supplication in the Spirit, being watchful to this end with all perseverance and supplication for all the saints..." **Ephesians 6:10-18**

Both letters to the churches at Corinth and Ephesus express a certain knowledge of the will of God regarding the lives we live in this world. Scripture is clear believers are going to contend with the kingdom of darkness in one form or another, whether *"...resisting the devil..." (**I Peter 5:8,9**)* or *"...wrestling against principalities, powers, rulers of the darkness of this age, or spiritual hosts of wickedness in heavenly places..." (**Ephesians 6:12**)* while we live in this world.

This would be a daunting, even frightening, task if we did not know *"...He who is in you is greater than he who is in the world..." (**I John 4:4**)*. Even though the weapons of our warfare are mighty in God, we must follow Jesus' example in the manner of our warfare. The example of Jesus being tempted by Satan in the wilderness helps us establish a Scriptural precedent for our warfare. The priority of our warfare is to gain knowledge of the truth and to sustain that knowledge in faith, simplicity, and patience. *No wild tirades against the devil!*

As we grow in the knowledge of God we will learn of the provisions He has given us as His sons. All provisions of the new covenant must be appropriated and operated by faith; they do not come to us nor operate automatically. When we meet resistance, it will most surely be motivated by the thief. Jesus told us how to identify the thief: *"The thief does not come except to steal, and to kill, and to destroy." **John 10:10.***

Whenever we are pressed upon by anyone or anything trying to *"...take away..."* any of the provisions of the new covenant, we can identify that as the work of the thief. Jesus came to provide us with abundant life, not take life away from us. **Simple!** Just keep it simple by doing what Jesus did in His temptation and we will win, but there will be a fight, make no mistake about it!

Measure everything anyone wants to teach you as the will of God with the written standard provided in Scripture, Holy Spirit affirmation, and confirmation from the brethren who are approved unto God able to rightly divide the word of truth. As we have already stated and restated again, *"Our priority is to exercise faith according to our knowledge of the will of God. Certainty of the will of God will bolster our faith against any stimulus trying to promote doubt."*

Chapter Eight
Diversity of Methods

The New Testament presents a diversity of methods by which people can receive healing. Some of those methods are: *"...Laying on of hands, the spoken word, gifts of healings, miracles of healings, special healings, casting out spirits of infirmity, elders praying the prayer of faith, confessing your faults to one another..."*. Although there are a diversity of methods, the source of healing in the new covenant is the eternal redemption obtained by the blood of the Lamb no matter what method is used to receive healing. If the source of healing in the new covenant is constant, then why are there a diversity of methods involved in healing? Consider Jesus healing several men of blindness during His earthly ministry to provide at least one answer to this question.

1. ***In two healings Jesus***, *"...touched their eyes, saying, 'According to your faith let it be to you.' And their eyes were opened..."*
 (Matthew 9:29,30).

2. ***In another healing***, *"...one was brought to Him who was demon-possessed, blind and mute; and He (Jesus) healed him, so that the blind and mute man both spoke and saw..."*
 (Matthew 12:22).

3. ***In the healing of Blind Bartimaeus Jesus asked***, *"...'What do you want Me to do for you?' The blind man said to Him, 'Rabboni, that I may receive my sight.' Then Jesus said to him, 'Go your way; your faith has made you well.' And immediately he received his sight... **(Mark 10:46-52)***.

Lord of Healing

4. In still another healing, *"...He took the blind man by the hand and led him out of the town. And when He had spit on his eyes and put His hands on him, He asked him if he saw anything. And he looked up and said, 'I see men like trees, walking.' Then He put His hands on his eyes again and made him look up. And he was restored and saw everyone clearly..."* **(Mark 8:22-26)**.

5. And finally, *"...He spat on the ground and made clay with the saliva; and He anointed the eyes of the blind man with the clay. And He said to him, 'Go, wash in the pool of Siloam' (which is translated, Sent). So he went and washed, and came back seeing..."* **(John 9:1-12)**.

In all six healings the result was the same, blind men received their sight. Why did Jesus employ different methods even though all produced the same result? We find a clue in Mark's record of Jesus ministering in His own country.

> *"Then He went out from there and came to His own country, and His disciples followed Him. And when the Sabbath had come, He began to teach in the synagogue. And many hearing Him were astonished, saying, 'Where did this Man get these things? And what wisdom is this which is given to Him, that such mighty works are performed by His hands! Is this not the carpenter, the Son of Mary, and brother of James, Joses, Judas, and Simon? And are not His sisters here with us?' So they were offended at Him. But Jesus said to them, 'A prophet is not without honor except in his own country, among his own relatives, and in his own house.'* **Now He could do no mighty work there, except that He laid His hands on a few sick people and healed them. And He marveled because of their unbelief...**" Mark 6:1-6

This clue reveals a powerfully important understanding identifying a link between Jesus' **ability** to *"...do mighty work..."* for the people and the faith of the people. Mark wrote

Diversity of Methods

*"...Jesus **could do** no mighty work there..."*. Mark did **not** write *"...Jesus **would do** no might work there..."*. The difference between *"...could..."* and *"...would..."* is enormous.

Just imagine, *"...unbelief..."* of the people **stopped** the power of God from flowing out of Jesus so He, *"...**could do** no mighty work there..."*! How is that possible, that any condition of **man** could stop the power of **God**? Yet according to Scripture inspired by God the Holy Spirit, that is exactly what happened. Jesus *"...**could do no mighty work there**, except that He laid hands on a few sick people and healed them. And He marveled **because of their unbelief**..."*.

Isn't that putting an unrealistic and unbearable pressure on people, that Jesus will not move among them if they have *"...unbelief..."*? It is not that Jesus *will not* move among them, but rather He *cannot* move among them! In this dispensation Jesus cannot impose the will of the Father on people. There is a time coming when *"...He shall rule them (the nations) with a rod of iron..." (**Revelation 2:27**)*, but that time is not now. Now, people have to willingly receive God's will in order to partake of it.

Two pieces of revelation are needed to answer the question whether a faith requirement is unrealistic and unbearable. **The first is:** *"Faith comes by hearing, and hearing by the word of God."* **Romans 10:17**. *"For by grace you have been saved through faith, and that not of yourselves; it is the gift of God, not of works, lest anyone should boast."* **Ephesians 2:8,9**. Jesus the Living Word clothed in flesh was standing right there in the midst of the people of

His own country. The living presence of the word created an opportunity for faith to be readily available to anyone who would have turned their heart toward God to receive the faith which *"...comes by hearing, and hearing by the word of God..."!*

The second piece of revelation is: The people chose to see Jesus only as *"... the carpenter, the Son of Mary, and brother of James, Joses, Judas, and Simon? And are not His sisters here with us?"*, rejecting Him as the Living Word. Their refusal to turn their hearts toward God placed a veil over their hearts keeping them from being able to see Jesus as the Living Word *(II Corinthians 3:12-18)!* Scripture is clear in this matter, the people did not believe. *"...He (Jesus) marveled because of their unbelief..." (Mark 6:6).* As we have already seen in *Chapter Four...*

> ***Unbelief is a conscious choice!***

Why is *"...faith..."* so important? The disgustingly deceptive enemy has subtly and craftily used his devices in an effort to corrupt our understanding of this most holy gift! Faith is not something you have to manufacture nor something in which you have to be *"...man enough..."* or *"...good enough..."* to walk! Faith is a gift from God which *"...comes by hearing, and hearing by the word of God!" **Romans 10:17**.*

The new covenant operates by faith. Faith is divinely empowered ability given to us so we will be able to enter the new covenant, live in it, and partake of the provisions of it. ***Faith is a gift!*** The only ways ***not*** to have faith are either to

Diversity of Methods

have not heard the word necessary to receive it or to have heard and rejected the Word, just as the people of Jesus' own home country did. Such actions will thwart the will of God! Faith is important because it is the means by which God has chosen the new covenant to operate!

> ***Our main concern ought to be why anyone would reject this holy gift from God?***

The Holy Spirit inspired the writer of the letter to the Hebrews to write, *"...without faith it is impossible to please Him (God)..." (Hebrews 11:6)*. How could God inspire any writer to write such? ...Because God will give faith to anyone who will receive it *(Romans 10:13-17)*. Without faith it is impossible to please Him because without faith a person will not be able to partake of eternal life. God is pleased when a person receives life, but not pleased when a person misses life. ***Life is the real issue!*** Faith is just the gift through which He makes life available. Any quality of life less than new covenant life in which a person walks is not pleasing to God, especially since God provides faith as a gift for a person to partake of better. So, *"...without faith it is impossible to please Him..." (Hebrews 11:6)*.

No matter which *"...method..."* Jesus used, the *"...faith..."* of each blind man was a necessary part of the healing process. In Jesus' own country the *"...unbelief..."* of the people ***stopped*** the power of God from flowing out of Jesus to them. Jesus desired for the blind men to have faith so He could heal them.

Lord of Healing

In the first two healings Jesus said, *"... 'According to your faith let it be to you.' And their eyes were opened..." (**Matthew 9:29,30**)*. In the healing of Blind Bartimaeus Jesus said, *"... 'Go your way; your faith has made you well.' And immediately he received his sight..." (**Mark 10:46-52**)*. In the healings involving *"...spit..."* can you imagine the faith it took for the blind man to have accepted Jesus' method of spitting on his eyes or the faith it took for the other blind man allowing Jesus to anoint his eyes with clay made from spit and dirt, and, then, still blind, follow Jesus' instructions to go wash his eyes in the Pool of Siloam? In all six healings the *"...faith..."* of the blind men was necessary in order for Jesus to be able to heal their eyes.

The various methods Jesus employed in each healing served the purpose of helping to *"...provoke..."* the blind men to faith so He could heal them. Scripture says, *"...let us consider one another in order to stir up (**NKJV**) (to provoke one another unto [**KJV**]) love and good works..." (**Hebrews 10:24**)*. God sent His only begotten Son into the world to save the world because He desires the world to be saved! However, faith is the means God has chosen for man to partake of salvation, that includes healing. He will not impose His will on anyone! **Faith is required!** Jesus' actions helped to *"...stir up or provoke..."* these blind men to faith so they could be healed.

The Sovereign Triune God is the source of the plan of salvation. Clothing the Second Person of the Trinity in flesh and sending Him to the earth to be born of a virgin, to live as a man, to shed His blood in death to provide an eternal redemption all originated from within the heart of God! The

Diversity of Methods

new covenant is God's idea. Man was not involved in the planning, development, nor giving of the new covenant. Every facet of the new covenant is an expression of God's love to redeem us from the power of darkness, deliver us into the kingdom of His dear Son, make us His sons, and give us access to Him as our Father. All of these things are God's idea not men's.

We do not have to talk God into making provision for us! He desires to make provision for us! Even when we exceed the limits of our faith and need His mercies, *"...they are new every morning..." (**Lamentations 3:22,23**)*. God is the Alpha and the Omega! He loves us and desires only good for us.

> *"For I know the thoughts that I think toward you, says the Lord, thoughts of peace and not of evil, to give you a future and a hope."* ***Jeremiah 29:11***

It is inconceivable to think such a God who would give His only begotten Son to be *"...The Lamb of God who takes away the sin of the world..." (**John 1:29**)* would leave us to our own devices against infirmities, sicknesses, and diseases. Even the medical community defines these conditions as *"...harmful deviations from normal..."*. Anyone who has ever suffered from infirmity, sickness, or disease knows how much they are like *"...the thief who does not come except to steal, and to kill, and to destroy..." (**John 10:10**)*. Our loving benevolent Father went to extraordinary lengths to make provision for our spirits. He has done the same for our bodies. *"...you are not your own? For you were bought at a price; therefore glorify God in your body and in your spirit, which are God's..."* ***I Corinthians 6:19,20***

Lord of Healing

Scripture is clear our God *"...desires all men to be saved and to come to the knowledge of the truth..." (I Timothy 2:4)*. Paul wrote to the church at Rome that *"...whoever calls on the name of the Lord shall be saved..."* but then asked, *"...How then shall they call on Him in whom they have not believed? And how shall they believe in Him of whom they have not heard? And how shall they hear without a preacher? And how shall they preach unless they are sent?..." (**Romans 10:13-17**)*. After Jesus' resurrection from the dead and just prior to His ascension into heaven He commanded,

> *"All authority has been given to Me in heaven and on earth. **Go therefore and make disciples of all nations**, baptizing them in the name of the Father and of the Son and of the Holy Spirit, teaching them to observe all things that I have commanded you; and lo, I am with you always, even to the end of the age."* **Matthew 28:18-20**

God *"...desires all men to be saved and to come to the knowledge of the truth..."* and is willing to send us to the nations to give them opportunity to know Jesus so they may believe in Him in order to be saved. We must tell people Jesus' shed blood is what obtained the eternal redemption for their spirit and their body. God is sending us to tell all nations of the redeeming work of Christ!

No matter which method may be employed for people to receive healing, the source of all of them in the new covenant is the eternal redemption obtained by the blood of the Lamb. In the same manner that God *"...desires all men to be saved and to come to the knowledge of the truth..."*, so, too, He desires for us to be healed. Every method by which we may be healed, whether *"...laying on of hands, the spoken word, gifts of healings,*

Diversity of Methods

miracles of healings, special healings, casting out spirits of infirmity, elders praying the prayer of faith, or confessing your faults to one another...", they are all God's provision for us. God desires for us to be delivered from anything and everything which involves the power of darkness stealing, killing, or destroying any part of us! Just as in the process leading to new birth a person must come to the knowledge of the truth in order to be saved, so, too, in the process leading to healing a person must come to the knowledge of the truth in order to be healed. A diversity of methods by which we may be healed are merely God's provision for us given because He loves us!

Lord of Healing

Chapter Nine
What if...?

What if you embrace *"...sound doctrine..."* regarding *"...healing..."*, accept Christ as Healer, exercise your faith to receive healing, and it doesn't work like you think it should?! It is not my intent to hinder the faith you have received from hearing, or in this case, reading revelation of the word of God. However, I desire to help you avoid many of the pitfalls into which I was taken captive in my walk of faith.

Healing is absolutely the will of God, a fundamental part of the eternal redemption obtained by the blood of the Lamb shed at the time of His death! No one can change that irrefutable fact and immutable truth! However, it is also an historical fact from modern church history that many people have aborted their faith through doubt and unbelief because *"...things did not work the way they thought they should..."*. As we have already seen, external stimuli can promote doubt which becomes the doorway to unbelief.

"...Mail-box..." faith is not the will of God. That is, quoting Scripture, *"...my God, shall supply all your need according to His riches in glory by Christ Jesus..."* **(Philippians 4:19)** then running to the mail-box every day looking for your *"...need to be met..."*. Under these conditions when the *"...need..."* is not met, a person generally aborts their faith. Mail-box faith is not the divinely empowered gift from God given for the purpose of entering the new covenant, living in it, and partaking of the provisions of it.

Lord of Healing

Have you ever heard the story, whether true or not I cannot say, about a man who lived in an area which flooded. He had to climb on the roof of his house to avoid the water while he waited in faith for the Lord to deliver him. He waited right up to the time he drowned. When he arrived in heaven, he asked the Lord what happened. The Lord replied, *"I sent a boat and a helicopter."* I suppose the man refused the boat and the helicopter thinking they could not possibly be the Lord's provision. We do not get to decide how the Lord will meet our need!

A more *"...healing..."* appropriate illustration will help move us toward understanding the operation of faith to receive healing. Suppose your head begins to ache and you take some remedy from a pharmaceutical company. Upon taking the remedy, your head continues to ache. You do not immediately *throw-in-the-towel* complaining the remedy did not work. You understand there is some time delay in order for the remedy to produce the result you seek. Even in pain you patiently wait for relief because you understand the remedy is not immediate.

Suppose we learn sound doctrine regarding healing, accept Christ as Healer, and begin to exercise our faith to receive healing for some ailment in our body. Perhaps this particular ailment has pain accompanying it. The pain does not instantly go away with the exercise of our faith, and, so, we begin to doubt. If the pain continues, our doubt becomes the doorway through which we pass into unbelief. We abort our faith because the healing does not manifest itself quickly

What if...?

enough. It is not within our prerogative to determine the time frame in which healing will manifest in our body.

How long do we have to wait? It is essential that we have revelation of healing and understanding of how *"...process..."* is a part of healing before we actually try to appropriate healing. Until you have grown sufficiently in your understanding of healing as a provision of the new covenant, in most cases it would be better for you to seek help from the medical community. **Seeking medical attention is not anti-Christ!** Our God finds no pleasure in our being sick or in pain. He desires for us to be free from infirmities, sicknesses, and diseases.

The enemy has persuaded many precious sons of God that if they do not receive healing by faith but, rather, have to seek medical attention, they are *"...less than..."* in God's eyes and in the Christian community. What a blatant, insidious, and destructive device! Having just made such dramatic statements, we must qualify them with a Scriptural based precedent.

Faith *can be* contrasted with doubt and unbelief. However, a person may not have faith because he has not heard the word in order to have received faith. If a person does not have faith because he has **rejected** the word he has heard, his rejection of the word is *"...unbelief...".* Doubt is uncertainty about the word, but unbelief is a conscious choice not to believe the word. In settings involving Jesus during His earthly ministry, He frequently encountered persons who rejected the word, refusing to believe. Scripture records some of His most scathing rebukes in such settings.

Lord of Healing

In Matthew's record of Jesus casting out a demon from a man's son whom His disciples could not help, we find just such a rebuke.

> *"...Jesus said to them, O faithless and perverse generation, how long shall I be with you? How long shall I bear with you?..."* **Matthew 17:17**

Jesus also rebuked His disciples for doubt and unbelief. When Peter chose to walk out to Jesus on the water, then doubted and began to sink, Jesus rebuked him saying, *"O you of little faith, why did you doubt?" (Matthew 14:31)*. It is extremely important to draw a stark contrast between a person not having faith because he has not heard the word and a person not having faith because he has chosen to consciously reject the word.

If we have turned our heart toward the Lord which will remove the veils keeping us from seeing Christ allowing us to behold the glory of the Lord, our faith will be solidly based on the Christ we see. That is what makes doubt and unbelief which overrides faith in a person who has already received faith so corrupt: A person to whom faith has already come allows something to rise above the knowledge revealed to him by God. Consider what Paul wrote in his second letter to the church at Corinth.

> *"For though we walk in the flesh (that is, a body made of flesh), we do not war according to the flesh. For the weapons of our warfare are not carnal (of the flesh) but mighty in God for pulling down strongholds, casting down arguments and every high thing that exalts itself*

What if...?

against the knowledge of God, bringing every thought into captivity to the obedience of Christ, and being ready to punish all disobedience when your obedience is fulfilled." **II Corinthians 10:3-6**

According to this Scripture, God has given us powerful weapons able to pull down any stronghold or cast down any argument or any high thing that exalts itself against our knowledge of God and to bring every thought into captivity to the obedience of Christ. If *"...faith..."* has come to us as a result of our having heard the word and yet we allow a stronghold, an argument, or some high thing to exalt itself against the knowledge of the word we have received, it is because we have chosen to reject what we have heard and not to believe it. Unbelief is a conscious choice. These actions are corrupt.

Faith is a gift from God! *"Faith comes by hearing, and hearing by the word of God."* **Romans 10:17**. The only requirement necessary for a person to be able to receive faith is for that person to turn his heart toward the Lord when he hears the word! God engineered the new covenant to be based on the divinely empowered ability *(...faith...)* that He would freely give man as opposed to the old covenant which was based on man's own ability. The new covenant is based on better promises than the old covenant and *"...is..."* better than the old covenant *(Hebrews 8:6,7)!*

It is easy to see the Lord's perspective regarding a person consciously rejecting the word and choosing not to believe. He still loves such a person, but He will not change His design allowing unbelief to become an integral part of this holy covenant put in force by the death of His only begotten

Son! The new covenant is a faith based covenant, and faith is a provision from God for all who will receive it!

In order for a person to have faith to receive healing, he must believe in Christ as Healer. In order to believe in Christ as Healer, he must hear of Him. In order to hear of Him, someone must preach to him. In order for someone to preach to him, he must be sent to do so. This is sound doctrine based on Scriptural precedent *(see **Romans 10:13-17**)*. As we have already stated, this Scriptural precedent does not exclude a person studying and hearing from the Holy Spirit on his own to receive faith.

Once faith has come as a result of our having heard the word, we must *"...keep our heart with all diligence for out of it are the issues of life..." (**Proverbs 4:23**)*. We must not allow anything or anyone to promote doubt and certainly not unbelief in our hearts. We need to remain steadfast and unwavering in our faith!

Everyone, absolutely everyone, who receives Jesus and is born again, enters the church as a *"...babe in Christ..." (**I Peter 1:22-2:3**)*: Whether the person is a scholar, a captain of industry, a leader of a nation, or greatly successful in some natural endeavor in life, everyone becomes a *"...babe in Christ..."* at the time of his new birth. ***No exceptions!***

When Peter wrote *"...as newborn babes, desire the pure milk of the word, that you may grow thereby..." (**I Peter 2:2**)*, he expressed a concept we all must understand. It is the will of God for all members of the body of Christ to grow! As we begin to grow as a babe, our growth will not immediately propel us into adulthood in the spirit. As we grow we will pass through the stages of growth parallel to those in the natural world. We will grow from babe to little child to young man to adult. Just as natural babes require parental oversight so, too, spiritual babes require parental oversight and guidance to help them grow through the various stages in the most efficient manner. Included in this parenting process is *"...stewardship..." (I Corinthians 4:1,2)*, provision of proper diet at the proper time and in the proper manner.

Paul wrote some very provocative thoughts from the perspective of a person who had successfully passed through childhood into manhood. These terms could apply to both realms, natural and spiritual.

> *"When I was a child, I spoke as a child, I understood as a child, I thought as a child; but when I became a man, I put away childish things."* **I Corinthians 13:11**

It is not always pleasant to remember *"...when I was a child..."*, but it is necessary and very helpful. Remembering *"...when I was a child..."* will surely evoke memories of behavior commensurate with a child. Behavior such as impatience and selfishness. Adult input leading a child to maturity is designed to teach the child how to *"...put away childish things..."*. Both natural and spiritual children must learn they do not get everything they want; and even things they need often must be patiently awaited. These skills are essential for successfully appropriating the provisions of the new covenant by faith.

Lord of Healing

Do you remember some of the things we learned as children? Some of the things were just *"...foolish..."*. Things like, *"Don't swallow your bubble gum. It will stay inside you forever." "Don't cross your eyes. Someone may come up behind you, hit you on the back while you have your eyes crossed, and they will stay that way forever."* Other things were superstitions. Things like, *"Don't walk under a ladder or break a mirror. That is bad luck." "Don't walk in the same direction where a black cat just crossed in front of you. Bad luck."* Other things were, well, I don't know, you decide. *"Smoking is not bad for you, Uncle So-in-So smoked all his life and he lived to be 100 years old." "Margarine is good for you, butter is bad for you." "Butter is good for you, margarine is bad for you."* **What is truth?** This question is an age old philosophical debate.

For Christians, truth is not what but, rather, who: **Christ is Truth!** Yet the world, even much of the church world, has debated Christ for generations. It seems the debaters have been persuaded everyone has a right to their own opinion in this debate. This persuasion comes from people who are endeavoring to *"...see..."* Christ with their natural abilities. Scripture is perfectly clear, *"Eye has not seen, nor ear heard, nor have entered into the heart of man the things which God has prepared for those who love Him. But God has revealed them to us through His Spirit..."* **(I Corinthians 2:9,10)**. Anyone who turns their heart toward the Lord will have any veil that has hindered them from seeing Christ taken away, and they will behold the glory of the Lord **(II Corinthians 3:16-18)**. Anyone who refuses to turn their heart toward the Lord will continue to debate...

What if...?

These debates cause great challenges in our lives. The content of the debates often becomes *"...tradition..."* or even worse *"...doctrine..."* in our midst. Scripture recorded Jesus telling certain scribes and Pharisees *"...you have made the commandment of God of no effect by your tradition. Hypocrites!..." (**Matthew 15:6,7**)*. Some of the mind-sets of the debaters are: *"God has given us doctors as His means for us to be healed." "God put this dreadful disease on you to teach you something." "Sister So-in-so died from sickness and you know if healing was God's will, He would have healed her. She was the most godly woman I ever met." "Well, I prayed for God to heal this person, and they were not healed. If God would have wanted this person healed, He would have answered my prayer."* These mind-sets and others like them have become the *"...tradition..."* and *"...doctrine..."* by which many live.

Jesus said, *"I am the way, the truth, and the life." (**John 14:6**)*. No man defines Christ! Certainly no tradition or doctrine of man can change who Christ is. What if you have determined whether healing was the will of God or not on the basis of some of the mind-sets of the debaters? What if *"...tradition and doctrine of men..."* have become the way you live? There is no tradition, no doctrine, no condition from which we cannot be set free. Jesus came to *"...deliver us from the power of darkness..." (**Colossians 1:13**)*. All that is required is for us to turn our heart toward the Lord, and then when we receive any input from anyone, we will know whether it is Truth! It is time for us to *"....put away childish things..."!*

Lord of Healing

Chapter Ten
Spirits of Infirmity

Throughout history man has passed through a vast array of mind-sets concerning the way we live. Many of the modern era see these changes as transition out of the age of darkness into the age of enlightenment. Truly there were some mind-sets based on superstitions, vain imaginations, and traditions handed down from one generation to another that needed to be left behind: For example, the mind-set that the earth was flat. The work of scholars enhanced by daring explorers forced man to abandon the flat earth notion, leaving only the unreasonable and argumentative to hold such. Albert Einstein's Theory of Relativity challenged Sir Isaac Newton's laws of physics and changed the way man saw the entire universe. This change was based on provable mathematical calculations.

A great many people who entered this *"...age of enlightenment..."* deemed any thought not scientific, academic, or intellectual in nature to be only for the superstitious, uneducated, or foolish. An extremely dangerous mind-set began to emerge: *If a thing cannot be proven by scientific means, then it either is not real or does not exist.* **For everyone who is a Christian this is completely unacceptable!** God is a Spirit *(John 4:24)* and cannot be scrutinized by the strict scientific, academic, or intellectual standard. That is not to say God cannot be experienced, just not in the crucible of the scientific, academic, or intellectual.

This dangerous mind-set continues even today. There is a controversial movie currently being shown entitled, **God is Not Dead**. The storyline of the movie follows the notion that everything must be measured by the scientific, academic, or intellectual standard in order to be acceptable. Paul wrote by inspiration of God the Holy Spirit in his second letter to the church at Corinth regarding this very matter.

> *"Therefore we do not lose heart. Even though our outward man is perishing, yet the inward man is being renewed day by day. For our light affliction, which is but for a moment, is working for us a far more exceeding and eternal weight of glory, while we do not look at the things which are seen, but at the things which are not seen. For the things which are seen are temporary, but the things which are not seen are eternal."*
> **II Corinthians 4:16-18**

Here Paul identified two worlds, the visible natural world which is temporary and the invisible spiritual world which is eternal. We understand the world continues to be divided over two distinctly differing views regarding the universe. One view believes that everything came from a *"...big bang..."* and a process of *"...evolution..."*. The other view believes God created man in His own image and placed him in the universe He Himself had made. The fundamental difference between these views seems to be oriented to the existence of the spirit world.

The only way to walk successfully with God is by faith. *"But without faith it is impossible to please Him, for he who comes to God must believe that He is (exists), and that He is a rewarder of those who diligently seek Him."* **Hebrews 11:6.** Faith is a gift from God

Spirits of Infirmity

(Ephesians 2:8,9) which comes to anyone who hears the word *(Romans 10:17)* with his heart turned toward the Lord *(II Corinthians 3:16-18)*. A person cannot be persuaded that God is the Creator; he must believe it by faith.

God is not asking us to believe just anything and everything! He provides us with a revelation of Himself and the divinely empowered ability to see, understand, and walk in that revelation. God has given us a covenant, a new covenant based on the ability He provides, not our own ability. He is asking us to walk in the faith He gives in agreement with Him, His word, and His will. Every person must choose to believe the existence of only a natural world or both a natural world and a spiritual world!

One of the mind-sets of the distant past included acceptance by many that the spiritual world was as real as the natural world. Contained in the spiritual world are both good and evil beings. Satan and all the demons of his kingdom are spirit beings who live in the spirit world. During Jesus' earthly ministry both He and His disciples cast demons out of people. *Mark* and *Luke* give account of a demon possessed man from the country of the Gadarenes *(Mark 5:1-20 & Luke 8:26-39)*. *Mark* records Jesus speaking directly to the demon saying, *"Come out of the man, unclean spirit!" (Mark 5:8)*. Later in this same account *Mark* records the demons speaking directly to Jesus saying, *"...Send us to the swine, that we may enter them..." (Mark 5:12)*.

In this particular case the demons were not just influencing this man from an external position, they were living inside of him. When cast out, the demons went to live inside of the swine. Demon spirits living inside of a person will have a variety of different effects on the person in whom they inhabit according to the particular *"...type..."* of demon they are. *Mark* records Jesus healing people who were blind, mute, and deaf with the source of their conditions being demonic. Here is one such record of Jesus healing a boy who had a *"...deaf and dumb spirit...".*

> *"And when He came to the disciples, He saw a great multitude around them, and scribes disputing with them. Immediately, when they saw Him, all the people were greatly amazed, and running to Him, greeted Him. And He asked the scribes, 'What are you discussing with them?' Then one of the crowd answered and said, 'Teacher,* **I brought You my son, who has a mute spirit. And wherever it seizes him, it throws him down; he foams at the mouth, gnashes his teeth, and becomes rigid.** *So I spoke to Your disciples, that they should cast it out, but they could not.' He answered him and said, 'O faithless generation, how long shall I be with you? How long shall I bear with you? Bring him to Me.' Then they brought him to Him. And when he saw Him, immediately the spirit convulsed him, and he fell on the ground and wallowed, foaming at the mouth. So He asked his father, 'How long has this been happening to him?' And he said, From childhood. And often he has thrown him both into the fire and into the water to destroy him. But if You can do anything, have compassion on us and help us.' Jesus said to him, 'If you can believe, all things are possible to him who believes.' Immediately the father of the child cried out and said with tears, 'Lord, I believe; help my unbelief!' When Jesus saw that the people came running together, He rebuked the unclean spirit, saying to it:* **'Deaf and dumb spirit, I command you, come out of him and enter him no more!' Then the spirit cried out, convulsed him greatly, and came out of him.** *And*

Spirits of Infirmity

he became as one dead, so that many said, 'He is dead.' But Jesus took him by the hand and lifted him up, and he arose..." **Mark 9:14-27**

Perhaps we might consider this boy's father to have been superstitious, uneducated, or unenlightened because he said his son had a *"...mute spirit..."*. However, when Jesus interacted with the spirit identifying it as a *"...deaf and dumb spirit..."*, we understand it was a living being from the spirit world. The boy received deliverance so that when the demon went out of him, the boy could hear and speak. If we say the boy had an infirmity, sickness, or disease, we must do so in an extended sense. The boy had a demon. Jesus did not pray for him to be healed. Jesus cast out the demon making the boy free from the effects of the demon.

Matthew also recorded Jesus helping a man's son be freed of a demon. While most probably it is the same account of which *Mark* wrote, the terminology is different.

> *"...And when they had come to the multitude, a man came to Him, kneeling down to Him and saying, 'Lord, have mercy on my son, for he is an epileptic and suffers severely; for he often falls into the fire and often into the water. So I brought him to Your disciples, but they could not cure him.' The Jesus answered and said, 'O faithless and perverse generation, how long shall I be with you? How long shall I bear with you? Bring him here to Me.' And Jesus rebuked the demon, and it came out of him; and the child was cured from that very hour."*
> **Matthew 17:14-18**

The accounts are just too similar for there to have been two different men both having sons with these demonic conditions. However, even though they are most likely two records of the same account, the differences are striking. *Mark's* record provides significant detail more than *Matthew's*. The boy's father describes the condition differently in each account, and even though *Mark* and *Matthew* use different terms, both record the source of the condition as *"...demonic..."*. *Matthew* told us only that *"...Jesus rebuked the demon, and it came out of him; and the child was cured from that very hour..."*.

Mark records the father's view of the demon as *"...throwing his son into the fire and into the water to destroy him..."*, revealing demonic intent. *Mark* also reveals the demon's response to Jesus' command to *"...come out of the boy and enter him no more..."*, *"...the spirit cried out, convulsed the boy greatly, and came out of him..."*. When Jesus told the demon to *"...enter the boy no more..."*, the implication is the demon could have entered the boy again had Jesus not prohibited it. One last detail *Mark* provided is most important. After the demon had come out of the boy, the boy *"...became as one dead, so that many said, 'He is dead.'..."*.

Because the vast majority of the church on the earth today have all but forsaken the possibility of demonic activity in man, any information we gain from Scripture is extremely helpful to boost our understanding. Even though Jesus had authority over this demon, the demon was still able to *"...convulse the boy greatly..."* before it came out of him leaving the boy *"...as one dead..."*. Even after the boy was delivered of the demon, the boy needed ministry. *"...Jesus took the boy by the hand and lifted him up, and he arose..."* from a condition that appeared *"...as dead..."*.

Spirits of Infirmity

There was much involved in the process of providing deliverance for this boy: Jesus identifying a *"...spirit..."* as the source of the boy's condition and being led to cast the demon out as the solution required. On the way out of the boy the demon *"...convulsed the boy greatly..."*, and the boy *"...became as one dead..."* requiring additional ministry. If we are going to participate in deliverance for people we must add to our knowledge that the source of some infirmities in people may be demonic. As we have already seen, these conditions can parallel natural infirmities, sicknesses, and diseases, such as a person being blind, deaf, or mute. In these cases praying for the person to be healed will most likely be ineffective because the real need is for a demon to be cast out. Jesus did not pray for this boy to be healed; He cast out a demon and the boy was *"...cured from that very hour..." **(Matthew 17:18)***.

I remember an account of deliverance told by a minister who provided *"...the prayer of faith..." **(James 5:15)*** and *"...laying on of hands..." **(Hebrews 6:2)*** for the infirmed as part of his ministry. He recalled a time while praying for the sick after a certain meeting in which he had preached. A woman desiring ministry told him the medical community had diagnosed her condition as tuberculosis. She said every *"...healing evangelist..."* in the country had prayed for her, but none of them could help her. As this minister began to pray for her, he said the Holy Spirit showed him in the spirit a small creature holding onto the top part of one of her lungs. He was made to understand this was a spirit which would have to be cast out in order for the woman to be made whole. So, he commanded the spirit to come out of her. The spirit came out of her, and she was completely *free*. Even though everyone said she had been healed, the source of her freedom came from being delivered from the demon spirit. The minister did not pray for her to be healed; he cast out a demon spirit from her, and she stopped suffering from the demonic affects.

Every infirmity, sickness, or disease does not have a demon as its source, but some do! If a demon is *not* involved, we simply pray for the sick using one of the means identified in Scripture. If a demon *is* involved, we cast it out. *This leads us to an important question:* **How do we know if a demon is involved or not?** Jesus' earthly ministry illustrates how he knew...

During His earthly ministry He did not arbitrarily determine what to do to help a person in need. Jesus said, *"...Most assuredly, I say to you, the Son can do nothing of Himself, but what He sees the Father do; for whatever He does, the Son also does in like manner..." (**John 5:19**)*. Jesus repeated this concept just a few verses later, *"...I can of Myself do nothing. As I hear, I judge; and My judgment is righteous, because I do not seek My own will but the will of the Father who sent Me..." (**John 5:30**)*. Every part of Jesus' earthly ministry was a direct result of being guided by His Father.

In **Chapter Five** we considered Jesus *"...healing..."* several men of blindness. Although all six men were blind desiring to receive their sight, Jesus used a diversity of methods including deliverance to help them. If we build on the premise that Jesus' entire ministry was *"...not to seek His own will but the will of the Father who sent Him..."* then, the diversity of methods

Spirits of Infirmity

He employed to heal the six blind men were what the Father willed. Jesus knew whether to cast out a demon or pray for healing because He was led by the Holy Spirit who showed Him the Father's will.

After six years as members of Wycliffe Bible Translators, four of those years in Papua New Guinea as translation personnel, my wife and I resigned from Wycliffe and returned to the USA to begin a new phase of ministry. This new ministry would involve ministering from the pulpit and praying for the sick. In the process of starting this new ministry, the Holy Spirit instructed me to ask Him if I was to pray for the sick before I actually prayed. At first I did not understand how this instruction could possibly be from God! I was fully persuaded *"...healing..."* was the will of God, so why would I need to ask anything before praying for the sick to be healed! However, I was certain this instruction had come from the Holy Spirit, so I followed His guidance.

As I began to pray for the sick, I carefully and purposefully consulted the Holy Spirit before I prayed for every person. If I did not receive any instructions, I would lay on hands and pray the prayer of faith. On one particular occasion, following this pattern, a woman came forward to receive ministry and the Holy Spirit said, *"She is full of bitterness. Ask her if she will repent."* The Holy Spirit even showed me the person about whom the woman was bitter. I did as the Holy Spirit had shown, consulted the woman about being bitter, and asked her if she would repent. She acknowledged the bitterness and repented. I was released to lay hands on her and began to pray the prayer of faith. She instantly received a verifiable healing. Everyone rejoiced!

In another instance in a foreign land, a teenage girl had suffered from meningitis as a child leaving her unable to hear or speak. Following the pattern of asking before I prayed, the Holy Spirit showed me this was a spirit which must be cast out in order for the teenager to be freed. When I had successfully cast out the demon, no one needed to ask whether the teenager was free. Her face began to shine and her eyes sparkled. She was hearing the sound of the praise and worship team as they played in the background. The first words she learned were, *"Praise the Lord"!* It was a tender and holy moment!

There is a diversity of methods by which a person may be *"...healed..."* or *"...delivered..."* as the case may be. However, the diversity is not within our prerogative but, rather, the will of God. He does not will diversity just to spice things up, His will is focused on the *"...way..."* to help a person be free from the power of darkness which holds them captive. If the person has a *"...spirit of infirmity..."* such as the *"...deaf and dumb spirit..."* Jesus cast out of the man's son (**Mark 9:14-27 and Matthew 17:14-18)**, our priority is to cast out the spirit. If a demon is not involved, we employ one of the diversity of Scriptural methods of healing. ***The choice is the Holy Spirit's, not ours!***

Summary & Conclusion

Anyone who has ever suffered the ill effects of infirmities, sicknesses, or diseases does not need to be convinced how dreadful they are. Even the common cold is disgusting. Annual global spending on prescription drugs is in the billions of dollars. The whole world is seeking relief from infirmities, sicknesses, and diseases.

Jesus' contrast of Himself with the thief perfectly describes the intent of the enemy.

> *"...The thief does not come except to steal, and to kill, and to destroy. I am come that they may have life, and that they may have it more abundantly..."* **John 10:10**

The man whose son needed deliverance described the actions of the *"...mute spirit..."* in his son: *"...often he has thrown him both into the fire and into the water* **to destroy him***..." (Mark 9:22)*. Demonic intent *"...to destroy..."* is a perfect match of the intent of *"...the thief..."*! While Satan as *"...the thief..."* is certainly not the source of every infirmity, sickness, or disease, surely we can see infirmities, sicknesses, and diseases convey the same intent: *They steal, kill, and destroy.*

The magnificent work of Christ providing salvation is *"...finished..."*! Now all anyone has to do to be saved is appropriate the finished work of Christ! In the same manner, Christ's magnificent work providing healing is *"...finished..."*! Now all a person has to do in order to be healed is appropriate the finished work of Christ!

The new covenant is a covenant of *"...faith..."!* Every provision of it is only able to be seen, understood, and appropriated by faith. Paul was inspired to write a very curious thing to the troubled church at Corinth. Writing about *"...order in church meetings..."*, he wrote:

> *"If anyone thinks himself to be a prophet or spiritual, let him acknowledge that the things which I write to you are the commandments of the Lord. But if anyone is ignorant, let him be ignorant."* **I Corinthians 14:37,38**

During Jesus' earthly ministry He was a perfect expression of the Father and all the Father willed. He never spoke carnally minded. He never spoke out of human frustration, anger, or bitterness. He always spoke the word, the will, and the way of the Father. Nevertheless, many to whom He was sent refused the simplicity and the majesty of His ministry.

When I first began in ministry, I was so naive. I knew Jesus repeatedly told His disciples the way people treated Him was the way they, too, would be treated *(John 15:20)*. However, I was slow to accept the fact that people would reject an anointed, simple, and understandable presentation of *"...truth..."* and instead adhere to tradition or the doctrine of men without so much as a single question or consideration of faith. More than thirty-five years of ministry have taught me that many people who refuse truth will remain ignorant even though God desires more for them!

The Lord Jesus is asking everyone to turn their heart toward Him to consider any revelation of Him. With your

Summary & Conclusion

heart turned toward the Lord, exercise your faith to consider the revelation presented in this book to see if it conforms to Holy Scripture, is affirmed by the Holy Spirit, and confirmed by those who are approved unto God. God wills for men to be saved and healed! He has made provision for both.

This book is an offering of my office of ministry, the anointing I have received to freely obtain and freely give revelation of the Lord, and a simple understandable written format in which the revelation may be presented. It is my hope and prayer that you will turn your heart toward the Lord, ask questions, and study to see what is written in this book is revelation of Christ the Healer. In the end, my hope and prayer is that you may be healed of all your diseases!

www.ingramcontent.com/pod-product-compliance
Lightning Source LLC
Chambersburg PA
CBHW071301040426
42444CB00009B/1820